TWAYNE'S WORLD AUTHORS SERIES

A Survey of the World's Literature

FRANCE

Henry Becque

(TWAS 180)

TWAYNE'S WORLD AUTHORS SERIES (TWAS)

The purpose of TWAS is to survey the major writers—novelists, dramatists, historians, poets, philosophers, and critics—of the nations of the world. Among the national literatures covered are those of Australia, Canada, China, Eastern Europe, France, Germany, Greece, India, Italy, Japan, Latin America, New Zealand, Poland, Russia, Scandinavia, Spain, and the African nations, as well as Hebrew, Yiddish, and Latin Classical literatures. This survey is complemented by Twayne's United States Authors Series and English Authors Series.

The intent of each volume in these series is to present a critical-analytical study of the works of the writer; to include biographical and historical material that may be necessary for understanding, appreciation, and critical appraisal of the writer; and to present all material in clear, concise English—but not to vitiate the scholarly content of the work by doing so.

Henry Becque

By Lois Boe Hyslop

The Pennsylvania State University

Twayne Publishers, Inc. :: New York

Library of Congress Catalog Card Number: 74-147183

MANUFACTURED IN THE UNITED STATES OF AMERICA

FOR FRANCIS

Preface

In the glittering Paris of the Second Empire, with its hothouse atmosphere of luxury, frivolity, license, and frenzied gaiety, the theater seems to have epitomized the very life and spirit of the age. To a pleasure-seeking populace it offered the brilliant but superficial amusement which had become the very goal of its existence. Theaters of all kinds, including opera houses, concert halls, and *cafés-concerts,* catered to the tastes of the public. Drama, melodrama, light opera, serious opera, farce, comedy, and vaudeville became immensely popular, while remaining strictly secondary in artistic value and literary importance to the novel and to poetry.

Throughout the Second Empire and during the first years of the Third Republic, Paris flocked to see the social and moral dramas of Augier and Dumas *fils;* the witty, complicated plays of Scribe; and the melodramas, vaudevilles, and comedies of Sardou. Of no less interest were the comedies and light dramas of Pailleron and Gondinet, as well as the hilarious farces and comedies of Labiche. But nowhere did the pleasure-loving spirit of the Second Empire find better expression than in the madly gay operettas of Offenbach with their infectious melodies, their frenetic rhythms, and the irreverent wit and irony furnished by the most successful of his collaborators, Meilhac and Halévy.

In the 1870s, after the fall of the Empire, Augier, Dumas *fils*, and Sardou continued to dominate the theater, although new currents were gradually making themselves evident. Coppée, Banville, Bornier, and Mendès—to mention only a few—met with only limited success in their attempt to impose poetic fantasy on the stage, in part because, as André Antoine points out, they were obscured by the brilliant revival of Hugo's dramas after his return from exile.

The Naturalists proved no more successful than the poets in taking over the theater. As early as 1865 the Goncourts' *Henriette Maréchal* met with disastrous failure; in 1873 Zola's *Thérèse Raquin* was withdrawn after nine performances. If *L'Assommoir,* adapted by Busnach and Gastineau, attracted widespread attention in 1879, it was largely the result of the public's curiosity.

After 1880, while the Naturalists were still trying unsuccessfully to gain control of the stage, an obscure writer by the name of Henry Becque produced two plays, *Les Corbeaux (The Vultures)* and *La Parisienne (Woman of Paris),* whose sobriety and uncompromising realism stood in sharp contrast to the artificiality and spurious wit of the *pièce bien faite* (well-made play) popularized by Scribe. At that time almost no one suspected that the struggling, little known artist was to give a new direction to the contemporary theater and that his two plays would one day rank among the few real masterpieces of nineteenth-century French drama.

It will be the aim of this book not only to relate Becque to the Realistic theater which immediately preceded him and to Naturalistic drama which he is often said to have initiated, but also to discover what constitutes his originality and makes him one of the most important playwrights of the nineteenth century. At the same time, it is the intention of the present writer to take note of his esthetic ideas and critical judgments and to relate them to the critical thought of his time.

The originality of Becque and the nature of his accomplishments can best be measured by a careful analysis and evaluation of his plays and critical opinions. Biographical facts, introduced in an opening chapter, are mainly restricted to those aspects of his life, career, and temperament that are relevant to an understanding of the man and his work. It is noteworthy that in the last years of his life Becque's influence was exerted not so much through his theater as through his lectures, his newspaper articles, and his role as a literary lion in the fashionable salons of the day.

Minor plays, most of which have been deservedly forgotten, are briefly discussed in chronological order with the intention of showing the development of Becque's technique and the growth of his originality. An entire chapter is devoted to each of the two plays on which his reputation rests and to his esthetic ideas and criticism, which only recently have begun to receive a small amount of attention.

On the other hand, discussion of his poetry has been deliberately omitted. At its best, it shows a sincerity and melancholy that are often moving; more often than not, it is little more than rhymed prose with none of the dazzling virtuosity that he so admired in Victor Hugo or the "suggestive magic" that Baudelaire and the Symbolists had introduced into poetry.

Like Musset in his independence and in his indifference to traditional practice, Becque holds a comparatively small but very important place in the evolution of French drama. Although his contribution is limited to but two plays and to the written and oral expression of his esthetic ideas, he nevertheless effected a salutary change in the drama of his day by attacking its meretricious theatricality and by creating a drama that more closely resembled reality than that of either his predecessors or his contemporaries. The simplicity and naturalness of his technique, the integrity of his conception, and his ability to shape reality, while seeming to merely reproduce it, have made of him one of the pioneers of modern drama as well as the greatest and most powerful of Realistic dramatists in France.

LOIS BOE HYSLOP

The Pennsylvania State University

CONTENTS

Chronology

1837 April 18, Henry-François Becque is born in Paris at No. 20, rue de Chabrol to Alexandre-Louis Becque and to his wife Jeanne Martin.

1848 October, Becque enters the Lycée Bonaparte, later known as the Lycée Condorcet.

1854 Leaves the lycée without attempting to pass the *baccalauréat.* December, finds employment at the Northern Railway Company where he remains until August 19, 1856.

1860 January 20, Becque obtains a position at the Chancellery of the Légion d'Honneur through the influence of his brother Charles. September, resigns his position in hopes of becoming a writer and tries to earn a living first as a stockbroker and then as a tutor.

1865 Becque becomes the secretary of a Polish nobleman, Count Potocki, through whom he meets the young composer Victorien de Joncières.

1867 February 8, the opera *Sardanapale,* for which Becque wrote the libretto and Joncières the music, is produced at the Théâtre-Lyrique.

1868 November 6, *L'Enfant prodigue,* Becque's first play, is presented at the Vaudeville.

1870 June 17, *Michel Pauper* opens at the Porte Saint-Martin where it is staged at Becque's own expense. July 19, the Franco-Prussian War breaks out, and, a few weeks later, Becque enlists as a simple soldier and takes part in the siege of Paris.

1871 November 18, *L'Enlèvement* opens at the Vaudeville where it is given only five performances. Becque abandons the theater and resumes work at the Stock Exchange.

1872 July, revival of *Michel Pauper* at the Théâtre de Belleville. Becque may have begun writing *Les Corbeaux.*

1876 Becque serves as a writer and drama critic for the paper *Le Peuple* until June 5, 1877.

1878 November 15, *La Navette,* a one-act play, opens at the Gymnase.

1880 January 1, *Les Honnêtes Femmes,* a one-act play, opens at the Gymnase. March 14, revival of *L'Enfant prodigue.*

1881 Becque serves as drama critic for the paper *Henri IV* and later for the *Union Républicaine.* Death of Becque's father at age of eighty.

1882 September 14, *Les Corbeaux* is finally presented at the Comédie-Française after a period of years during which Becque had vainly sought a producer.

1884 March 11, death of Becque's mother (Robaglia mistakenly gives 1883).

1884 Becque contributes to *Le Matin.*

1885 February 7, *La Parisienne* is presented for the first time at the Renaissance with *Les Honnêtes Femmes* as a curtain raiser. December 21 to 29, a revival of *La Parisienne* played in conjunction with *La Navette.* After several performances, *La Parisienne* continues alone and plays before a full house each night until January 6, 1886.

1886 February 26, revival of *La Navette* at the Renaissance. October 27, revival of *Les Honnêtes Femmes* at the Comédie-Française. The most popular of Becque's plays during his lifetime, it is also performed in 1887, 1888, 1889, 1890, 1892, and 1893. December 15, revival of *Michel Pauper* at the Odéon with Paul Mounet as Michel. December 28, Becque becomes a chevalier of the Légion d'Honneur. Writes for *La Revue Illustrée* from 1886 to 1888.

1887 Becque begins work on *Les Polichinelles.*

1888 Becque writes for *Le Gaulois, Le Figaro* and *La Revue Illustrée.* June 7, *La Parisienne* is performed in the salon of Madame Aubernon with Réjane as Clotilde and Antoine as Lafont.

1890 November 11, an unsuccessful revival of *La Parisienne* at the Comédie-Française. November 14, death of Becque's sister Aimée-Caroline who had married Jules-Marie-Antonin Cyr after the death of her first husband, Ernest Pierre-Maria Salva. Publication of Becque's *Théâtre complet* (2 vols.) by Charpentier and of *Querelles littéraires* by Dentu. Becomes a candidate for the French Academy but loses to Charles de Freycinet.

1891 October 31, *La Parisienne* is performed in Marseilles at the Théâtre des Variétés.

1893 Becque is invited to Milan and to Rome where he is fêted by the Italians and honored by performances of *La Parisienne* and *Les Corbeaux.* December 18, a brilliant revival of *La Parisienne* at the Vaudeville with Réjane as Clotilde.

1894 March 17, death of Becque's brother Charles. July 1, Becque is granted a pension of twelve hundred francs by the decree of the Minister of Public Instruction and Fine Arts. December, is invited to speak in Liège and in Brussels.

1895 Becque becomes guardian of two small grandnephews following the death of his niece Jeanne Salva in 1893 and that of her husband Georges Robaglia in 1895. November 27, Becque is honored at a festival in Marseilles where he lectures on the contemporary theater and attends a highly successful performance of *La Parisienne* with Antoine as Lafont. Publication of *Souvenirs d'un auteur dramatique.*

1896 June 27, publication of *Madeleine,* a scene from *Les Polichinelles,* in *La Vie Parisienne.* February, Becque is invited to speak in Copenhagen and in Holland. May, Becque is again a candidate for the French Academy. Loses to André Theuriet.

1897 January 23, publishes *Veuve!* in *La Vie Parisienne.* March 20, publishes *Le Domino à Quatre* in *La Vie Parisienne.* May 1, publishes *Le Départ* in the *Revue de Paris* and *L'Enlèvement* in the *Revue du Palais.* July 24, publishes *Une Exécution* in *La Vie Parisienne.* July 27, is promoted to *officier* of the Légion d'Honneur. November 3, revival of *Les Corbeaux* at the Odéon.

1898 Becque's *Théâtre complet* (3 vols.) is published by the Société *La Plume.* May, revival of *La Navette* at the Théâtre des Capucines. Becque contributes to the paper *La Volonté.* December 3, publishes *Notes d'album* in *La Vie Parisienne.* Is a candidate for the French Academy but withdraws after the first ballot. Loses to Henry Lavedan.

1899 March, Becque helps stage his one-act play *Madeleine* which is played in the salon of Madame Lucien Muhlfeld. April 19, revival of *La Parisienne* at the Théâtre Antoine with Antoine as Lafont and Antoinette Legat as Clotilde. Becque had helped coach the actors, especially Suzanne Devoyod who succeeded Antoinette Legat in the role of Clotilde. April 4, Becque is left homeless and ill after a fire caused by his smoking in bed. After spending four days in the Maison Dubois, Becque is invited to the home of Paul Adam and his wife to recuperate. May 8, Becque returns to Paris and spends a miserable night in a hotel.

Enters the nursing home of Dr. Defaut in Neuilly after calling on Lucien Muhlfeld to come to his assistance. May 12, Becque dies at seven in the morning. May 15, is buried in the cemetery of Père-Lachaise, after funeral rites in the church of Saint-François-de-Sales, rue Brémontier, where many men of letters gather to honor him in death.

1904 A tombstone bearing the inscription "Henry Becque, dramatic author, 1837-1899" is placed on Becque's grave, bought by friends who had been approached by a committee composed of André Antoine, Emile Fabre, and Xavier Roux.

1908 June 1, a monument to Becque, presented by his friends to the city of Paris, is unveiled at the corner of the Avenue de Villiers and the Boulevard de Courcelles. The statue of Becque is based on the terra cotta bust made by Rodin in 1886. That evening *La Parisienne* with Réjane as Clotilde is played at the Odéon to a large and enthusiastic audience.

CHAPTER 1

Becque—the Man

I *Homo Duplex*

TO compare the frank, uncompromising criticism of Henry Becque and his violent, often scabrous attacks on his enemies with the warm portrait left by his close friends and by his grandnephew and editor, Jean Robaglia, is to discover that there were two Becques.[1] Behind the caustic, bitter, litiginous writer and critic known to the general public, there was another man seen only by his friends—sensitive, kind, warmhearted, hungry for affection—whose exuberance and boisterous good humor belied his alleged misanthropy. It was only in his last years that illness, poverty, and loneliness robbed him of the gaiety which he himself once called his most distinguishing trait.

A more paradoxical person could hardly be imagined. As a writer he wanted above all to be a lyric poet, yet his poetry is never read and is best forgotten. Though he devoted most of his life to the theater, he produced only two plays worthy of note. Yet both plays, each so different from the other that they seem not to have come from the same pen, broke with the conventional theater of the day and encouraged a group of younger writers to follow suit. Often hailed as the initiator of Naturalistic drama and of the *comédie rosse* (bitter and cynical comedy), he is in many respects closer to his literary idol, Molière, than to any other dramatist of the nineteenth century.

Though Becque compares favorably with Baudelaire and Flaubert as a critic and esthetician, his ideas on esthetics, surprisingly sound and independent, have gone more or less unrecognized, while his intemperate indictments of his contemporaries have received undue attention. Accused of immorality and of the bleakest pessimism, his plays contain not a single prurient line, and his personal beliefs were those of the solid, conservative bourgeoisie to which he belonged.

Criticized—often unjustly—for the violence of his hate, his one regret in his old age was his inability to have done all the good of which he had dreamed (VII, 243). During the last fifteen years of his life he was welcomed in fashionable literary salons where his gusto and sharp wit won him the adulation of the rich and socially prominent. Meanwhile, in his "attic" apartment he continued to live a life of poverty and misery, always in debt, yet eager to help those more in need than he.

Regarded as a misanthrope and a misogynist by the public, Becque had a deep affection for his friends, his supporters, and especially for his family. "I was always given love and support and shown the greatest indulgence by my admirable mother and all the members of my family," he once wrote to an unknown correspondent (VII, 241-42). And to his friend, Adrien Bernheim, who had recently lost his mother, he confided with moving simplicity: "The greatest sorrows, my friend, are not plays that fail, but places near the fireside that remain empty" (VII, 231-32).

In spite of his devotion to literature and, in particular, to the theater, he unabashedly considered the arts as secondary in importance to family, to politics, and to all that had to do with the welfare of his country: "Were it necessary to choose between the political and the literary activity of these past twenty-five years," Becque told an audience in 1896, "I have no hesitation; I attach more importance to the political activity" (VII, 93). Writing to a friend some seventy years earlier, Stendhal had attributed much the same sentiment to Molière: "I even believe that Molière, were he alive today, would prefer being a deputy to being a comic poet."[2] But the audience at the Odéon where Becque had been asked to speak preceding a performance of Aristophanes' *Plutus,* evidently thought otherwise. At this point in his lecture, Robaglia recounts, the boos and jeers became so loud that Becque was forced to leave the stage without finishing his remarks (VII, 94).

Becque himself was well aware of the contradictions in his nature and, in a letter to an unnamed correspondent who had evidently attempted an evaluation of the man and writer, he corrects what he considered certain misconceptions:

Your error is this: you make me out to be an artist, an unknown artist even. Perhaps I am an artist when I have a pen in my hand. But not for one moment longer. I immediately return to the mainstream of life; I would hate a life reduced to the proportions of a brotherhood and a specialty. I have neither the manners, the pretentions nor the usual narrowmindedness of an artist. My great passion has always been for my family and for each of its members. I have always believed in my country. I am a democrat with a liking for people. I put political activity above all others. I would rather be a soldier than a writer; I would gladly have become a banker (VII, 242).

II *From Clerk to Playwright*

Born in Paris on April 18, 1837, Henry Becque was one of three children born to Alexandre Becque, a bookkeeper of modest means, and his wife Jeanne Martin. The family life was a happy one, as Becque was to testify in one of his poems:

> And in the paternal home,
> Which sheltered me for so long;
> I was a gentle and loyal child,
> I filled it with gaiety.
>
> Et dans la maison paternelle,
> Qui m'a si longtemps abrité;
> J'étais l'enfant doux et fidèle,
> Je la remplissais de gaieté. (VII, 137)

Deeply attached to the members of his family and especially to his mother, Becque continued, even as a mature man, to turn to them for advice and aid.

At the lycée Bonaparte, Becque proved to be a rather ordinary student who, like many of his classmates, dreamed of becoming a poet. With his uncle, Pierre Martin, an obscure writer of vaudevilles known as Martin Lubize, he often attended the theater and soon became a fervent admirer of Molière. The close relationship between uncle and nephew lasted until the former's death in 1863 and did much to influence Becque in his determination to become a dramatist. Becque was never to forget their friendship and, until the end of his life, maintained that *Le Misanthrope et l'Auvergnat,* which Lubize had written in collaboration with Labiche, owed more to his uncle than to its more widely known coauthor.

To earn his livelihood, Becque found employment first at the Northern Railway Company and then at the Chancellery of the Legion of Honor where his brother Charles also held a position. Unable to adjust to the monotony of office life, he gave up his job and became a tutor in literature. In 1865 he became the secretary of a Polish nobleman, Count Potocki, through whom he made the acquaintance of Victorien de Joncières, a young composer, with whom he formed a close friendship that lasted until his death.

It was with Joncières that Becque produced his first theatrical work, the opera *Sardanapale,* for which he wrote the libretto. Based on a subject borrowed from Byron, the opera was produced on February 8, 1867 at the Théâtre Lyrique, one of four theaters in Paris devoted exclusively to serious and to light opera, so popular during the Second Empire. Becque himself was later to discount the importance of *Sardanapale,* and, though it survived sixteen performances, its modest success was largely due to the famous Swedish singer, Christine Nilsson, who sang the role of Myrrha.

Vaudeville was as popular as light opera during the Second Empire, and it is not surprising that Becque chose that genre for his first play, *L'Enfant prodigue (The Prodigal Son).* Thanks to the recommendation of Sardou, who had been kind enough to read the script, it was produced on November 6, 1868 at the Vaudeville where it proved moderately successful and prompted the critic Francisque Sarcey to note that its author possessed "that gift which takes the place of all others: gaiety."[3]

L'Enfant prodigue was followed by a more serious drama, *Michel Pauper,* which was refused both by the Comédie-Française and by the Porte Saint-Martin. At a time when Sardou, Augier, and Dumas *fils* had almost a monopoly of the Parisian theater, it was no small task for an unknown writer to find a theater and a director willing to run the risk of sponsoring his play. *Michel Pauper,* however, was finally accepted at the Odéon, but when it was put aside by the director in favor of plays that seemed more adapted to popular taste, Becque grew angry and impetuously started a suit against the theater. Unsuccessful in his attempt, he decided to stage the play at his own expense. After hiring the theater Porte Saint-Martin and engaging a troupe of actors headed by the famous artist Taillade, he himself directed the rehearsals and took charge of even the most minute details. *Michel Pauper* opened June 17, 1870 before a large and curious audience that gave the play a somewhat mixed reception. More famous for its author's stubborn courage and daring than for its own merits, it closed on July 6, and Becque was left with a debt of twelve thousand francs.

A few weeks later (July 19) the Franco-Prussian War broke out, and Becque, who enlisted as a simple soldier, took part in the siege of Paris. The war ended, he returned to the theater, determined to recoup his fortune. Working fast and furiously, he "dashed off," as he himself confessed, a three-act play, *L'Enlèvement (The Elopement),* which was produced at the Vaudeville on November 18, 1871. A thesis play in favor of divorce, much like those for which he so often condemned Dumas *fils, L'Enlèvement* proved to be a complete failure and was given only five performances.

Tired and discouraged, Becque withdrew from the theater for a few years and, badly in need of money, went back to work at the Stock Exchange where he gained information that proved valuable in writing *Les Polichinelles.* In 1876 Becque was made drama critic of *Le Peuple,* a newspaper founded by Floquet, which was so fanatically republican that it even reverted to the use of the revolutionary calendar. Becque's first article (March 11) was a review of a concert by Gounod, whom he roundly berated for his ostentation; his most severe commentary was a sharp indictment of de Vigny's *Chatterton,* which he had no hesitation in labeling "elementary and insipid" (V, 64).

It was also about this time that Becque undertook to write a new play–one which, he vowed, would avoid the faults of his earlier works and would come as close to perfection as possible. Becque made good his resolve, and the result was *Les Corbeaux (The Vultures),* one of the masterpieces of French literature. Though he spent what he called the happiest year of his life working on the play, his joy quickly turned to discouragement when he found that no theater in Paris was interested in the bleak drama, so unlike anything of that day.

Rather than make the changes requested by the various directors to whom he submitted the manuscript, Becque followed the advice of Sardou and left the play untouched. While marking time, he wrote two short one-act plays, both of which were presented with only modest success at the Gymnase: *La Navette (The Shuttle),* which opened on November 15, 1878, and *Les Honnêtes Femmes (The Respectable Women),* which was given for the first time on January 1, 1880. *La Navette,* a forerunner of *La Parisienne (Woman of Paris),* met with disapproval on the part of most critics, who associated it with the raw naturalism of Zola and his disciples; *Les Honnêtes Femmes,* a brief in favor of marriage and the "femme honnête," was almost entirely ignored, although it was later to become one of his most popular plays.

The comparative success of his two short plays only strengthened Becque's determination to find a producer for *Les Corbeaux.* Finally, through the intervention of Edouard Thierry, the director of the Arsenal Library and the former manager of the Comédie-Française, the long search came to an end. Thierry recommended the play to Perrin, his successor at the Comédie, who agreed to its production. As usual, Becque insisted on supervising the rehearsals, much to the consternation of the actors who were annoyed and unnerved by his acerbity and intransigence. But opposition died down when Perrin, after listening in secret to a rehearsal, advised the company: "Listen to him carefully; he is better at it than all of us" (I, 28).

Les Corbeaux opened on September 14, 1882. The house had been sold out to a public made curious by reports in the press and by Becque's reputation for nonconformity. The audience was made up of glittering notabilities, including Sarah Bernhardt; the actors were tense and nervous, fearful of shocking spectators long accustomed to the tried formulas of the *pièce bien faite*. At several points during the performance, exclamations and cries of disapproval arose, only to die down and give way to grudging admiration. The play was pronounced a success by the audience, though later performances were less favorably received. Critical reviews proved to be a mixture of praise and blame. Sarcey, in a series of articles, admired its Molièresque power on the one hand and, on the other, criticized its black pessimism. Louis Ganderax of the influential *Revue des Deux Mondes,* Henry Bauër, an ardent champion of Zola and the Naturalists, and Edouard Thierry were among those who hailed it as an undeniable masterpiece.

When the play was discontinued after eighteen performances, Becque's stature as a dramatist could no longer be denied. With *Les Corbeaux* he was accepted by the younger generation of dramatists as their leader and, until his death in 1899, he continued to receive the adulation of a small group of admirers and disciples.

The following year Becque set to work on a new play which was to prove even more astonishing than *Les Corbeaux.* After two years of intense work during which he wrote and rewrote the dialogue, he read the finished product, *La Parisienne,* to the critic Louis Ganderax and to the popular comic actor of the Comédie-Française, Edmond Got. Acting on their advice, he submitted the manuscript to the Comédie where the celebrated actor Coquelin proved to be as enthusiastic as he had been critical of *Les Corbeaux.* When, despite his recommendation, *La Parisienne* was rejected by the reading committee, Coquelin brought the play to the attention of the Vaudeville where it was likewise rejected. Becque was about to lose all hope when it was finally accepted at the Renaissance by a young actor, Louveau, who, under the name of Fernand Samuel, had recently taken over the theater.

On February 7, 1885, *La Parisienne* was presented for the first time at the Renaissance. The comedy was greeted with the usual salvos of praise and condemnation. J. J. Weiss, drama critic for the *Journal des Débats,* sharply attacked the play; Sarcey hedged with a sort of vague praise. The new school of young writers who were soon to center around Antoine and the Théâtre-Libre were unanimous in their unqualified approval and support; no one was more enthusiastic and ardent in his defense of Becque than Octave Mirbeau. Zola himself is said to have proclaimed the play a masterpiece. Despite reports that the play lacked action and that it was immoral in its outlook, *La Parisienne* proved a great success with the public and was given sixty-one performances.

La Parisienne was the last play that Becque was to offer the theater. Thenceforth the stage was to see only revivals of his work. In 1886, the Comedie-Francaise accepted *Les Honnetes Femmes* as part of its permanent repertory and in 1890, encouraged by Sarcey, it undertook a presentation of *La Parisienne.* Unfortunately, the comedy met with almost complete failure, caused mainly by the inadequate interpretation of actors accustomed to the "grand manner" of the Classical school.

In his account of *La Parisienne* (III, 120), Becque relates in detail his grievances against Claretie, the director of the Comédie, whom he accused of deliberately betraying his play with the help and encouragement of Sarcey, who had once again changed his mind. It was André Antoine of the Théâtre-Libre who finally came to the rescue and, in a letter to Sarcey, published in *Le Temps* on November 24, 1890, blamed the failure of *La Parisienne* on the acting and the stage setting. The grandiose decor and the highly dramatic and artificial diction, so unsuited to the tone of the play, were chiefly responsible for the lack of success, he affirmed, and his opinion was echoed by other critics, including Jules Lemaître. Three years later in 1893, Antoine was proved right when Réjane in the role of Clotilde triumphed in a brilliant revival of the play given at the Vaudeville.

Meanwhile, the sudden death of Becque's sister Aimée in 1890 came as a stunning blow to the dramatist and made the failure of his play seem trifling in comparison. An article by Sarcey implying that *La Parisienne* would prove financially unsuccessful soon roused him from his lethargy and sent him into a towering rage. Claiming that, in thus disparaging his play, Sarcey had discouraged the public from attending, Becque threatened the critic with a lawsuit but only succeeded in making himself a target for newspaper gossip. Though he later dropped the suit, he was never to forgive Sarcey, and his attacks on his enemy grew ever more violent and ruthless.

La Parisienne was revived on a number of different occasions and knew its greatest triumph with the celebrated Réjane in the role of Clotilde. On April 19, 1899, a few weeks before Becque's death, it was successfully performed at the Théâtre-Antoine with Antoine and Antoinette Legat playing the roles of Lafont and Clotilde.

Of all his plays, Becque's favorite was *Les Corbeaux*, and it was no secret that he hoped to see the play produced a second time. Through the intervention of some of his friends in the theater, his wish was realized and, on November 3, 1897, *Les Corbeaux* was revived at the Odéon. Ill health and fatigue had made the author less aggressive and combative, and though he faithfully attended the rehearsals, he proved far less demanding in his attempts to coach the actors or direct the action. Wearing a coat over his dress suit, ready to go on to dine at some fashionable salon, he would urge the artists not to be intimidated by his presence and not to act any "more solemnly" on that account.

The play had only a small success, and it was only through the efforts of Paul Ginisty and André Antoine, who had recently been made directors of the Odéon, that it reached its twentieth performance. It was then that Becque, refusing to take advantage of his friends, asked that the play be withdrawn—the only time in the annals of the theater that such a gesture had been made, as Ginisty is said to have remarked (I, 36).

Soon after completing *La Parisienne,* Becque began work on what was to have been his most ambitious play, *Les Polichinelles (The Puppets),* an ironic five-act play portraying the world of finance. In spite of the eagerness shown by directors to obtain production rights to the play and in spite of the encouragement of his admirers, Becque was unable to finish the work, though he worked on it intermittently for some fifteen years. His loyal friend, Antoine of the Théâtre-Libre, invited him to spend several summers at Camaret in Brittany where he and a few friends, together with their families, would often go for their vacations. Despite their hope that, without worries or distractions, Becque would be able to complete the manuscript, little or no progress was made. At his death in 1899, *Les Polichinelles* was found in its unfinished and fragmentary state—a series of unconnected scenes with no real thread to tie them together.

In the midst of his struggle to complete *Les Polichinelles,* Becque evidently attempted to give dramatic form to other subjects by which he was intrigued. In a notation found in his *Souvenirs* and dated July 4, 1893, André Antoine tells of one such effort: "As Becque and I were returning along the Champs-Elysées this evening—a beautiful starry night—he recited to me bits of a one-act verse play which he says he has just finished. It is the story of a young Symbolist poet introduced into a middle-class home, and after each long speech, Becque's powerful laughter rang out gaily into the night."[4]

Robert de Flers also recalls having heard Becque recite lines from what was evidently the same play, as they walked home late one night after spending the evening in the salon of Madame Aubernon (VII, 157). In the *Oeuvres Complètes* of Becque (Crès edition), Robaglia reproduces over two hundred lines of an unfinished act which he maintains consists of fragments of the play to which Antoine and de Flers refer.

It is difficult to form any valid judgment about the fragments. The wit seems crude and labored, and Becque has not even bothered to distinguish between the various speakers. One is left with the impression that, at this late date in his career, Becque was being far more influenced by his colleagues among the Naturalists than they by him.

Included in the edition of the *Théâtre Complet* of Becque, issued by La Plume in 1898, are five additional one-act plays which had been published separately in various journals in 1896 and 1897: *Madeleine,* taken from a scene in *Les Polichinelles; Veuve! (Widowed!),* a sequel to *La Parisienne; Le Domino à Quatre (Dominos for Four); L'Exécution;* and *Le Départ (The Departure).* All are too short, too insignificant to add anything to Becque's stature as a dramatist.

III *Later Years*

During the last twelve years of his life, Becque devoted most of his time to lecturing and to writing for various newspapers. Over a period of years he contributed articles to a large number of papers, most of which he republished, together with his lectures, in *Querelles littéraires* (1890) and in *Souvenirs d'un auteur dramatique* (1895). Unable to submit to the routine and discipline of a journalistic career, he moved from one journal to another, among them: *Le Gaulois* (1888), *La Revue Illustrée* (1886-88), *Gil Blas* (1893), *Le Journal* (1893), and *Le Figaro* (intermittently from 1888 to 1894). It was in some of these papers that, between 1888 and 1898, he published under the title of *Notes d'album,* the maxims whose sardonic humor and biting irony seem that of a nineteenth-century La Rochefoucauld.

Becque's reputation as a dramatist and literary critic spread outside of France even before he was well known in his own country. During the last years of his life, he was invited on a number of occasions to lecture abroad. In 1894 he spoke in Liège and in Brussels, and in 1896 he was invited to lecture in Holland and in Denmark where he appeared on the same program with Georg Brandes.

But it was in Italy (1893) especially that Becque received a warm and friendly reception that he was never to forget. Both in Milan and in Rome he was fêted by his admirers and accorded enthusiastic ovations at performances of *Les Corbeaux, La Parisienne,* and *Les Honnêtes Femmes.* Despite the fact that at the end of the trip his impresario absconded with the money, Becque was left with some of the happiest memories of his life. Nor were the Italians soon to forget the author of *Les Corbeaux* and *La Parisienne.* In 1908, nine years after his death when, on the initiative of Antoine, Sardou, and Emile Fabre, a bust of Becque was erected at the corner of the Avenue de Villiers and the Boulevard de Courcelles, a group of Italian men of letters were among those whose contributions helped pay for the monument.

After the success of *La Parisienne,* Becque suddenly became the rage of the intellectual salons of Paris where his sharp wit, his reputation as a misanthrope, and his brilliant and amusing conversation never failed to attract an admiring audience. It was in the salon of Madame Aubernon de Nerville especially that Becque knew his greatest success. Curiously enough, Dumas *fils,* for whom Becque always had the greatest scorn, had been until then the center of attraction, but a break between Madame Aubernon and the author of *La Dame aux camélias* left Becque without a rival. It was in the salon of Madame Aubernon that Réjane first played the role of Clotilde, with Antoine as Lafont, and it was there that Becque held forth triumphantly, delighting his listeners with his barbed wit and pausing only long enough to punctuate his remarks with his well-known "hein?," "quoi?" and concluding with the usual "n'est-ce pas que c'est drôle?"

Back in his attic apartment Becque led a drab and lonely life. His lodging had always been furnished in much the same way and invariably contained, together with a few other meager possessions, an iron bed, a night table, a chair, a long plank on trestles that served as a work table, and a bookcase containing, among its volumes, the works of Victor Hugo and Molière. After an evening spent in the luxurious surroundings of fashionable society, Becque often hated to return to his dreary room and would walk the silent streets with one or two companions, talking animatedly and filling the night with his ringing laughter.

One by one he had lost the members of his family to whom he had remained so closely attached–his father in 1881, before he had won recognition as the author of *Les Corbeaux,* his mother in 1884, and his sister Aimée in 1890. During the last five years of his life, after the death of his brother Charles in 1894, Becque began to show the misanthropy which has so often been exaggerated by his critics. He had always been able to depend on his brother for financial assistance and at one point had even found it necessary to move into his quarters. After Charles's death, Becque was so destitute that his friends obtained for him a small government pension of twelve hundred francs which, added to the annual pension of a thousand francs granted by the Société des Auteurs, constituted his major resources until his death. Plagued by eczema and by stomach disorders aggravated by his poor diet, Becque lost much of the gaiety and zest for life for which he was known among his friends, and his wit became more corrosive and virulent.

Further tragedy came to him with the death of his niece Jeanne Salva, the only daughter of his sister Aimée. After her death in 1893, followed by that of her husband Georges Robaglia in 1895, Becque became the guardian of their two small children, the eldest of whom was only five. Though he dreamed of having the children live with him, he was obliged to put them in a boardinghouse in La Rochelle where he visited them as often as his health and financial situation permitted.

Becque showed the same warm affection for his young grand-nephews that he had for other members of his family, and the children looked forward eagerly to the visits of their *tonton* Henry who, arriving with pockets filled with small gifts, did much to bring happiness into the lives of the two small orphans. It was the elder of the two, Jean Robaglia, who edited the complete works of Henry Becque, published in seven volumes by Crès (1924-26), and who wrote the long preface which serves as the chief source of information about Becque's life.

IV *A Gay Misanthrope*

Despite the sadness and misfortune which filled his last years, it seems a mistake to categorize Becque as a confirmed pessimist who saw only evil and tragedy in the world about him. His own testimony, as well as that of his friends, offers evidence to the contrary. Not that his works and his sallies do not often suggest a certain misanthropy as well as misogyny. But one should not be deceived by the façade. Becque's talent best expressed itself in satire, irony, and caustic wit, and it was only natural for him to exploit that aspect of his genius. Moreover, Becque was by nature uncompromising and fearless, and his quick temper flared into anger in the face of dishonesty, infamy, and injustice. His mordant wit was the weapon he used in damning evil and setting the world to rights. Any bitterness on his part was linked, as his friend Robert de Flers pointed out, to a profound kindness which he took great pains to hide. The young writer, who was to become known for his gay satirical fantasies, recalls his conversations with Becque in *Deux Hommages,* published on the twenty-fifth anniversary of the dramatist's death: "This excellent man, laughing derisively, would make the most terrible remarks about people and things, but his pessimism had so much truculence, his misanthropy so much vigor that the final result was a healthy and sound joy. Compared to him, optimists committed to happiness seemed dull and gloomy."[5]

De Fler's statement admirably characterizes the vitriolic witticisms and the stinging retorts which delighted Becque's listeners in the salons which he frequented. Typical of his wit are some of the maxims published under the title *Notes d'album:*

Of course, people get married without knowing each other. Do you want marriage to disappear completely?

There are two kinds of women: those whom you compromise and those who compromise you.

The flood proved a failure; one man survived.

The unfortunate thing about equality is that we only want it with our superiors.

Man and woman go together like a ball and chain.

The truly well-bred man lives with his mistress but dies at home.

It is obvious that the maxims depend as much on their venom as on the concision and vigor of their expression. Devoted to more innocuous subjects, they lose much of their power and effectiveness. The few that express a more optimistic philosophy offer sufficient proof of that fact:

Duties make us happier than passions.

Life is a very difficult work of art, and it is already quite an accomplishment to succeed in certain of its aspects.

Speak to me of a hidden and unknown suffering. That is the one that I would like to relieve.

Robert de Flers was only one of Becque's many friends who has confirmed the truth of the last maxim: "He [Becque] was delighted by the legend of malevolence that surrounded him. He would say spiteful things out loud and do kindnesses in secret. When he was reminded of them, he would say, 'I forbid you to slander me.' And to prove he was right, he would start railing against one of three or four people, in what he called his 'private little game of slaughter.' "[6]

Others have testified to Becque's warm heart, to his fondness for family and friends, his kindness to struggling young authors, his geniality and exuberance. It is true that, in answer to Jean Bernard, editor of *Le Figaro,* who had asked a group of writers to recall their ideal at the age of twenty, he wrote with disarming and pathetic simplicity: "I had many dreams when I was twenty, when I was thirty, and even later. None has been realized" (VII, 229). But Bernard had asked the question in 1898, only a year before Becque's death, when the dramatist was feeling ill and depressed. Becque's answer must be weighed against those given in response to a long questionnaire that had been published six years earlier, in *La Revue Illustrée* (December 15, 1892). Among his responses, most of them humorous and even paradoxical, are a number which confirm the view that Becque was far from being a misanthrope:

> Chief character trait: gaiety.
> My favorite merit: conversation.
> My chief fault: chatter.
> My dream of happiness: that of others.
> My favorite names: the ones of those I have loved.
> What I despise most: lying.
> Present state of mind: peace.
> My motto: accept your fate.

A poem, which may well have been written about the same time, since he speaks of "living on *Les Corbeaux* and *La Parisienne,"* gives much the same picture of the writer:

> I have no more hope and I have no more hate,
> The passing years have softened painful griefs.
> I am taken for a bitter, brutal and frightful man;
> I live in quiet and serene peace.
>
> Je n'ai plus d'espérance et je n'ai plus de haine,
> Le temps s'est écoulé sur les deuils douloureux;
> Je passe pour un homme amer, brutal, affreux;
> Je vis dans une paix recueillie et sereine. (VII, 139)

Moreover, in spite of having been rejected three times by the French

Academy (in 1890, 1896, and 1898), Becque seems to have borne no rancor and to have consoled himself with the thought that his idol, Molière, had also gone unrecognized by that august body. Like Stendhal, he felt sure of obtaining posthumous fame. "No matter what they do, I shall have my statue some day," he would say to his friends as they returned from some evening affair.[7] To his great satisfaction, he was made a member of the Legion of Honor in 1883 and awarded the rosette in 1897.

Even in the last two or three years of his life, when he suffered from loneliness, ill health, and poverty, he still found pleasure in the company of his many friends who remained loyal to the end. Edmond Sée tells of seeing him for the last time at an evening party: "a child despite his years, intoxicated with pleasure, who amused himself in whirling and capering, his shirt puffed out beneath his vest, the tab of a suspender dangling, his eyes shining, his face scarlet, taking enormous delight in whisking around in a strenuous waltz a pretty, blond, and terrified dancer: Madame Rostand, who was not yet expecting *Cyrano*. . . ."[8]

Becque was even less a misogynist than a misanthrope, though there seems little doubt that in real life he must have experienced both unhappiness and disappointment in love. Robaglia mentions the fact that Becque had spoken in veiled terms to his friends about a young girl to whom he had been engaged when he was young, but whom he had dropped when he discovered she was "like the others" (I, 41).

Another story, first told by Henry Bauër and often repeated, is sometimes cited as an explanation of his cynical treatment of women, particularly in *La Parisienne*. According to Bauër, Becque had invited a beautiful and charming woman to his apartment for tea. In preparation he had taken the greatest pains and had even gone to the expense of buying flowers for the occasion. But Becque waited in vain. Only after a period of several hours did he learn from his concierge that the woman in question had come and gone. On discovering that Becque lived on the sixth floor, she had protested that it was too many steps to climb and had driven away in her carriage without bothering to leave a word of explanation for her impatient admirer.[9] If the story is true, it is surely more comic than tragic, and Becque must have told it to his friend Bauër with a certain amount of relish and rueful amusement. In itself, it is hardly sufficient basis for any deep-seated pessimism or cynicism on his part.

To read the poetry of Becque, however, is to discover that, far from being a woman hater, he was a highly sensitive man, tortured by an "immense need of love" (VII 143). Though he shows himself unusually reticent in his *Souvenirs* and in his correspondence, the poems are surprisingly personal and offer us a glimpse into his private life. At one point in his career–perhaps when he was writing *La Parisienne*–he seems to have had a liaison with a young working girl whom he discovered one day in a small restaurant poring over a novel of Victor Hugo. The poem that begins, "Farewell! that is all that is left for me to say," may well have been inspired by the same young girl and indicates that he found at least temporary happiness with her:

> The charming caprice of your youth in flower
> Filled my solitude and quieted my torture.
>
> I was unabashed and you without pride,
> And my poor lodging took on a holiday air
> When you appeared so gaily on the threshold.
>
> Le caprice charmant de ta jeunesse en fleurs
> Peuplait ma solitude et calmait mon martyre.
>
> J'étais sans embarras, comme toi sans orgueil,
> Et mon pauvre logis prenait des airs de fête
> Lorsque tu paraissais si gaiement sur le seuil. (VII, 141)

But a number of Becque's other love poems are quite different in tone and often reveal bitterness and angry despair. Several of his poems suggest a passionate love affair which had degenerated into hatred and left its author saddened and embittered. One or two are reminiscent of the cynical characters and situation in *La Parisienne.*

A sonnet, apparently written in Becque's last years, seems, however, to indicate the same serenity to which he had testified in the questionnaire of 1892 and in the poem that appears to date from that same period:

> O insidious charm of our last years!
> Our dreams are ended, our tasks finished;
> We expect nothing more from man and fate,
>
> Those who loved us are no more than dust and ashes;
> Our place is waiting in the cemetery,
> And quietly we prepare ourselves for death.

O Charme pénétrant des dernières années!
Les rêves sont finis, les tâches terminées;
Nous n'attendons plus rien des hommes et du sort,

Ceux qui nous ont aimés ne sont plus que poussière;
Notre place est déjà marquée au cimetière,
Et nous nous préparons doucement à la mort (VII, 146).

V *Death*

On April 4, 1899 Becque was awakened at four o'clock in the morning by suffocating smoke. He had fallen asleep while reading in bed and his cigar had started a fire which had been smoldering for several hours. Stopping only to throw on a coat, he rushed to the street to call for help. Fortunately, his papers and manuscripts were saved, but Becque himself, ill and suffering from shock, was left homeless. Knowing that he lacked the means to provide for himself, two of his friends, Lucien Muhlfeld and Edmond Rostand, took him to a nursing home, the Maison Dubois, where he stayed for a period of four days. A few days later, Paul Adam and his wife invited the dramatist to convalesce at their château near Juvisy where the coming of spring and the careful attentions of Madame Adam seemed to revive his spirits and restore his health.

Hungry for a sight of his old haunts, Becque suddenly decided to return to Paris without first informing his hosts. Too weak to care for himself, he was obliged to call upon his young friend Lucien Muhlfeld who came to his assistance and finally placed him in a nursing home in Neuilly.

From that time until his death, his friends gathered around him and took turns keeping him company, knowing how much he dreaded to be alone. The rest and spring air seemed at first to revive him; he even spoke of writing a play about nursing homes—"an amusing play," he quickly added. But he suddenly took a turn for the worse and, on May 12, he died at seven in the morning—four days before the death of his archenemy, Francisque Sarcey. His friends, who arrived a few hours later, covered his body with flowers.

At his death, Becque left a debt of fifty-three thousand francs and no money to take care of his burial. He had always been strongly opposed to cremation—he had even made it the subject of one of his newspaper articles in 1884—and his friends had assured him that his fears were groundless. Through the Société des Auteurs they obtained a burial place for him at Père-Lachaise where he was followed to his grave by his friends from the theater and the world of letters. So many flowers had been sent that a second carriage was needed to convey them.

His friends continued to show their loyalty long after his death. André Antoine took every opportunity to present Becque's plays, and his success did much to encourage the Comédie-Française to accept *La Parisienne* as part of its permanent repertory. It was also Antoine who, together with Emile Fabre and a group of distinguished men of letters, took the initiative in erecting a monument to the author of *Les Corbeaux.* On June 1, 1908, in a ceremony presided over by Clemenceau, the aging Sardou presented to the city of Paris a statue of Becque that had been modeled after a terra cotta bust made by Rodin in 1886.

Becque's prediction had come true. The statue which he had ruefully claimed would one day be his, stands today at the corner of the Avenue de Villiers, not far from where he had last lived and from the streets where he had strolled with his young friend Robert de Flers talking hopefully of the future. Death, kinder to Henry Becque than life, had finally brought him the recognition which for so many years had been only an illusive but sustaining dream.

CHAPTER 2

Apprenticeship

I Sardanapale

"*SARDANAPALE* doesn't count or counts only as a joke." Becque wrote in his account of *L'Enfant prodigue* (II, 127). He was neither exaggerating nor being overly modest, for nothing in the libretto suggests the dramatic skill and power that were later to reveal themselves in *Les Corbeaux* and *La Parisienne.* Yet *Sardanapale* is not without its importance, since it marked Becque's entrance into the theater and strengthened his determination to become a dramatist.

In 1865, Becque had become the secretary of Count Potocki, a Polish nobleman who, knowing Becque's interest in poetry, introduced him to Victorien de Joncières, a young musician and composer belonging to the Wagnerian school. It was the period of the Second Empire when opera was much in vogue in Paris, and Joncières had already composed *Hamlet,* a mediocre opera based on an adaptation of Shakespeare's play by Dumas *père.*

The two men became close friends and decided to seek fame and fortune by pooling their talents. In a shabby room which served as their living quarters as well as their studio, they set to work on an opera, *Sardanapale,* which, like Delacroix's famous painting, was inspired by Byron's well-known play. To prepare himself for the task, Becque read the works of Byron, either in the original or, more likely, in the translations (1822-25) of the ardent anglophile Amédée Pichot. At the same time, he studied the librettos of well-known operas and reread the historical poems of Béranger, the popular ballad-poet for whose topical verse he always retained a certain fondness.

Whether Becque or de Joncières chose the subject is not known. The cult of Byron, which had marked the Romantic period, was still strong in France and, after a brief period of decline, had met with a sort of revival both in Paris and in the provinces. In 1856 the Opéra had even presented *Le Corsaire,* a ballad-pantomime in three acts "adapted from Lord Byron." Neither Becque nor de Joncières could have escaped the fascination exerted by the Byronic hero and by the melancholy splendor of Byron's verse.

Both writer and composer must likewise have felt the powerful influence of Delacroix's *Sardanapale* exhibited for the first time in the Salon of 1827-28. The fact that de Joncières had first studied to be a painter and that he must have been aware of the many engravings inspired by the painting throws further light on the choice of subject.

Sardanapale was presented February 8, 1867 at the Théâtre-Lyrique, one of four theaters in Paris devoted to serious or to light opera. The work met with little success and was given only sixteen performances. Joncières was criticized for a score that seemed unsuited to the general tone of the opera; the libretto was more or less ignored, and Becque's name was even cited incorrectly in several reviews. Only the celebrated Swedish singer, Christine Nilsson, who sang the role of Myrrha, received the unqualified praise of the critics.

The opera hardly deserved better. The music was undistinguished, the libretto lacked power and originality, and the lines were flat and banal. As might be expected, Becque plainly lacked the creative imagination which would have allowed him to give epic grandeur or lyric beauty to so exotic and melodramatic a subject. Years later Becque would have liked his readers to believe that his libretto was no worse than others of its time. Writing in *Le Peuple* on April 11, 1876, he admits its mediocrity while implying it was more or less typical of the day: "Composers are much to be pitied. They lack librettos; they look far and wide for them and find only some very mediocre ones–*La Fiancée d'Abydos, Sardanapale* and so many others" (V, 11). Though there is much truth in Becque's assertion, his general condemnation is not altogether justified, especially if one compares *Sardanapale* to the operas of Wagner, Gounod, or Verdi. It is clear that poetry was not Becque's forte and that he had yet to find the medium which would allow him to give full expression to his genius.

II L'Enfant prodigue

It is only with *L'Enfant prodigue (The Prodigal Son),* a vaudeville produced in 1868, that Becque can be said to have definitely begun his career as a dramatist. Following in the footsteps of his uncle Martin Lubize, who had collaborated with Labiche in writing the well-known *Le Misanthrope et L'Auvergnat* (1852), Becque chose a genre that was much in vogue at the time and that had been cultivated with phenomenal success by his famous contemporary. Becque's play, in fact, may well have been partly inspired by Labiche's *La Cagnotte* (*The Kitty*) (1864), the saga of a group of provincials who decide to spend a day in Paris.

But where *La Cagnotte* is more strictly a vaudeville in which the comedy derives almost entirely from situation and from broad farcical humor based on action that is often reduced to buffoonery, *L'Enfant prodigue* moves more slowly and verges at times on a genuine comedy of manners or even a comedy of character. Moreover, unlike *La Cagnotte,* Becque has reduced the number of songs to one and introduced only six short stanzas, three of which have only two lines.[1] This difference in format may explain in part why *L'Enfant prodigue* is listed in both the Fasquelle and Crès editions as a comedy, while the earlier Plume edition describes it as a vaudeville. Becque himself, in his account of the play, refers to it as vaudeville (II, 127).

For some time, however, vaudeville had been moving away from the form it had assumed during the period of the First Empire and the Restoration when, perfected by Scribe, it had come to mean a gay frothy comedy of manners, partly farcical, partly topical. Usually restricted to one or sometimes two acts, it was written in prose and rhymed couplets, interspersed with songs. Under the Second Empire, vaudeville lost none of the immense popularity it had won for itself and continued to draw enthusiastic crowds at the Théâtre du Vaudeville and the Théâtre des Variétés. Music, however, grew less and less important, and emphasis was placed almost entirely on broad farcical humor, directed at the bourgeoisie and stemming from a series of ludicrous situations through which the characters were whisked with often riotous speed.

With no influential contacts in the theater, Becque was at a loss to find a producer for his vaudeville. To facilitate its acceptance, he asked the well-known critic Sarcey to read the play and pronounce judgment. Sarcey showed little interest and made it quite clear that he had no wish to be bothered by so obscure a writer. It was at this moment that Becque's intense dislike for Sarcey first began. Looking back over the years, he recalls his initial impression of the "goujat" (scoundrel), as he contemptuously calls him: "All the Sarcey that I have known was there: the lack of breeding, the brutal egoism, and that comic self-importance that I shall always find so amusing" (II, 29).

In the meantime, Harmant, director of the Vaudeville theater, agreed to produce *L'Enfant prodigue* and, in accord with his request, Becque shortened the play from five acts to four. After a further delay of three months, the anxious author grew impatient, and it was agreed that Sarcey should read the manuscript for final approval. Matters only grew worse when Becque discovered that the critic had not even taken the trouble to finish reading the play. In desperation, he submitted the comedy to Sardou, who not only gave his hearty approval but also recommended it to Harmant. Becque was never to forget Sardou's kindness and, throughout his life, had only the highest praise for the man and his work, despite the marked difference between the brilliant melodramas of his successful contemporary and the somber realism of *Les Corbeaux*.

L'Enfant prodigue was finally produced on November 6, 1868 at the Vaudeville, where it met with a very favorable reception. Becque was fortunate to have in his cast some of the most able and popular actors of the day who obviously did much to enhance the success of the play. The press on the whole greeted the work with enthusiasm and recognized in its author a new and genuine talent. Théophile Gautier in *Le Moniteur Universel* (November 23, 1868) praised the contagious humor of the vaudeville and approved its simplicity and its naturalness. One or two critics were perspicacious enough to see that Becque revealed a power of observation and a dramatic flair that made his play more than mere vaudeville and gave promise of future greatness.

Even Sarcey, carried away by admiration, wrote in *Le Temps* (November 9, 1868): "This young man has received from the theater's fairy godmother that gift which takes the place of all the others: gaiety" (I, 11). A strange and paradoxical beginning for a writer who was later to be blamed by that same critic for his bleak pessimism and his uncompromising realism! A number of years later, Sarcey was to take credit for having discovered *L'Enfant prodigue,* much to the disgust and annoyance of Becque. "Oh, I've known Becque for a long time," he was said to have remarked. "He brought me his first play. I'm the one who had *L'Enfant prodigue* produced" (II, 136).

The intrigue, though not especially original, is handled adroitly and with a great deal of comic verve. Théodore, a naïve young provincial, is sent by his family to Paris to pursue his studies. In Paris, he promptly becomes involved with Clarisse, the daughter of a concierge. Already experienced in the ways of the world, Clarisse succeeds in deceiving the innocent young man, who falls madly in love with the attractive young girl. Soon afterward, Delaunay, a notary and family acquaintance, arrives on a nostalgic visit, hoping to renew his relations with the young woman who had been his mistress while he was pursuing his studies some years before. Delaunay soon discovers that Clarisse is none other than the Amanda whose charms he had been unable to forget and that Théodore is his rival. Badly disillusioned, Théodore accuses Clarisse of duplicity but is completely duped by her "explanation" and ends by actually begging her forgiveness and praising her integrity.

In the meantime, Bernardin, the father of Théodore, arrives in Paris, suspecting that his son may already have succumbed to the temptations of a large city. On the train, he had been taken in by the wiles of Clarisse-Amanda who, he was led to believe, was a widow living alone in Paris. When prudently assuming the name of Azincourt, Bernardin comes to her apartment, ostensibly to return the birdcage which she had "inadvertently" left on the train, Clarisse introduces herself as Hélène de la Richardière, niece of General Château-Landry.

Complications arise when Théodore arrives unexpectedly and Clarisse introduces father and son to each other under fictitious names. Bernardin is properly horrified when Madame de la Richardière presents his son as a baron and whispers to him that the young man had been spending a fortune on a "princess" with whom he was infatuated. Théodore is equally horrified when, in a quick aside, Clarisse informs him that Monsieur Azincourt is really her father. Remembering that Clarisse had told him earlier that she was a natural child, Théodore assumes the worst and collapses on the divan in a state of shock. Certain that he is guilty of incest, he later tells his unsuspecting father that he is leaving for America to expiate the faults of his youth. "One would have to go back to the story of Oedipus to find a similar example of fatality," he explains to the bemused Bernardin (Act IV, sc. 14).

It is only when Bernardin later discovers Delaunay in the apartment of Clarisse that matters are straightened out, and the play finally ends with the three gullible provincials returning to Montélimar, somewhat wiser in the ways of the world than before.

With its broad humor and its slight intrigue depending on chance encounters, a portrait revealing the identity of Clarisse, and an anonymous letter, *L'Enfant prodigue* is more or less typical of the vaudeville of the day. But where the plays of a skillful vaudevillist such as Labiche show no letup in rapidity of movement or in power of invention, *L'Enfant prodigue* slows to the point that at times it almost ceases to be vaudeville.

Much of the first act, in which Théodore takes leave of his friends in Montélimar, contains delightful touches that demonstrate the author's power of observation. The provincial setting in which the characters are revealed in all their comic solemnity constitutes a sort of genre painting. The concierge's dinner in Act II is likewise more typical of a comedy of manners. The last two acts, however, which depend mainly on a complicated intrigue, are more strictly speaking vaudeville. Full of verve and sparkling with gaiety, they prove highly entertaining, though somewhat lacking in originality.

The comic element of *L'Enfant prodigue* depends to a great extent on its Gallic humor and on amusing lines and byplay that are sometimes rather banal or timeworn but are often surprisingly witty and original. At times, Becque introduces "gags" that both in thought and style recall the maxims which he was to publish many years later: "Women are like photographs: there is always an idiot who carefully preserves the negative, while clever people share the proofs" (Act IV, sc. 15); "Illusions about a woman whom one has loved are like rheumatism: one never completely recovers" (Act IV, sc. 11). At other times, the action or lines seem to look forward to scenes in *La Navette* or even *La Parisienne.* Comparable to the latter is the scene in which Théodore, vexed at being duped by Clarisse, is duped a second time and ends by retracting his angry words and begging for her forgiveness.

On the whole, the characters are two-dimensional–caricatures that suit the needs of the farcical action–though Clarisse with her mixture of naïveté and practicality prefigures to a small degree the Antonia of *La Navette.* Théodore is more or less a stock figure. But père Bernardin, like Monsieur Perrichon of Labiche, comes closer to being alive and, with his pompous manner and his endless clichés, offers a delightful satire on bourgeois manners and bourgeois hypocrisy. Especially amusing is the long moral lecture in Act I in which he warns his son against the two great evils of the world–journalists and courtesans–and keeps repeating with paternal solemnity, "abstain, Théodore, abstain!"

Though little or nothing in the play anticipates the somber power of *Les Corbeaux,* it clearly looks forward to *La Navette* and *La Parisienne* in its wealth of irony and wit and in its use of the theme of man's gullibility in the face of a clever and unscrupulous woman. Becque himself was evidently aware that the play was neither much inferior nor superior to the average vaudeville of its day. In his modest appraisal of *L'Enfant prodigue* made a number of years later, he recalls with approval the words of Sardou who had so kindly agreed to pass judgment on the manuscript " 'Your *Enfant prodigue* is very amusing' he told me on my arrival. He had found the right word and all that there was to say about my play" (II, 135).

III Michel Pauper

Spurred on by the critical success of *L'Enfant prodigue,* Becque turned to more serious drama and, with *Michel Pauper,* sought to rival the productions of such popular contemporary writers as Augier, Dumas *fils,* and Sardou. Theater directors, wary of the unknown, were hesitant to assume the financial risks of a work differing in so many respects from the conventional drama of the day, and Becque soon found himself stranded without any means of producing his play. The director of the Porte Saint-Martin claimed to be committed for as long as three years in advance, the reading committee of the Comédie-Française was polite but unanimous in its refusal.

When *Michel Pauper* was finally accepted at the Odéon, Becque's triumph quickly turned to disillusionment, for he soon discovered that its production was being indefinitely postponed while other plays were being given preference. It was at this time that Becque began a lawsuit against the Odéon which ended in failure and left him with no other recourse than to stage the play at his own expense–an unprecedented step that captured the imagination of the public and won the admiration of other frustrated playwrights.

Despite the lateness of the season and rumors of potential political difficulties, Becque hired the Porte Saint-Martin, persuaded the famous actor Taillade to act the part of Michel, and took upon himself the arduous role of director and producer. The play opened on June 17, 1870. Taillade, an actor in the grand manner, who had fallen heir to the romantic roles formerly played by the great Frederick Lemaître, did much to insure the success of the drama. The brilliance and verve of his acting provoked the admiration of critics and public alike and gave greater credibility to the extravagant character of Michel. Becque himself was hailed as a writer of promise and undeniable talent by critics like Barbey d'Aurevilly, Jules Janin, Albert Wolff, and Francisque Sarcey. True, *Michel Pauper* was justly criticized for its faulty structure, its brutal realism, and its black pessimism, but on the whole it proved a critical success, despite an audience that grew smaller each night as a result of a heat wave that overwhelmed the city. The play closed after eighteen performances when Taillade was forced to withdraw because of previous commitments. The last performance took place on July 6. On July 8 rumors of an impending war reached the city.

Michel Pauper is a ponderous drama in five acts. A workman, a chemist, and an inventor, Michel is associated with a rich industrialist, Monsieur de la Roseraye, who finds himself on the point of financial ruin after a life of debauchery and malpractice. Michel, who alone is conscious of Roseraye's dishonesty, falls in love at first sight with his employer's daughter Hélène, not knowing that she is infatuated with a dissipated young nobleman, the Count de Rivailles.

When Roseraye commits suicide after confessing his guilt to his long-suffering wife, Michel puts at the disposition of the widow and her daughter a small house which he had bought for himself. Michel's love for Hélène transforms him from a coarse, tippling workman into an inventor of genius, devoted to the cause of the laboring class. Stripped of her fortune and deserted by the Count who, though refusing marriage, had forced her to yield to him, Hélène agrees to marry Michel. On her wedding night, overcome by guilt in the face of Michel's adoration, she confesses her fault. Michel, in revulsion, strikes her and leaves, and Hélène in anger and desperation sends for the Count.

The last act of the play reveals Michel, his mind destroyed by alcoholism, tended by the devoted Madame de la Roseraye. Hélène returns, hoping to make honorable amends and to restore Michel to health. She has come too late. Michel dies without recognizing his wife, after first destroying the discovery that he had labored so long to make—the crystallization of carbon into diamonds.

Many influences can be seen at work in the play. The pathos, especially obvious in the monologue of Madame de la Roseraye at the beginning of Act II, recalls the *comédie larmoyante* (tearful comedy) of the eighteenth century, while the extravagantly passionate characters of Michel and Hélène, as well as the intrigue itself are suggestive of the Romanticism and melodrama of Victor Hugo. The fact that Becque made his hero a workingman and that, in a lengthy scene in Act IV, he briefly touches upon the problems of the laboring class is more closely related to the humanitarian tendencies of the Romantic movement after 1830 than to the social preoccupations of either Augier or Dumas *fils.* In fact, Michel, as Paul Blanchart has suggested, seems a sort of Ruy Blas of the scientific and revolutionary nineteenth century, but a Ruy Blas, it should be added, who is motivated by the conscience and the mentality of a Jean Valjean.[2]

Becque was very proud of "having centered around a romantic

intrigue all the demands that socialism was making at that time" and calls attention to the fact that he had shown "a concern for reforms and social justice which until that time had been foreign to the [French] theater" (VI, 103). Despite his distaste for the works of Dumas *fils* and Augier, he clearly reveals the influence of their drama both in his use of the *raisonneur* and of the long moral tirade. Not only does he introduce a *raisonneur* in the person of the noblehearted Baron Von-Der-Holweck, cousin of the Count de Rivailles, but he also indulges in moral preachments that outnumber those of *Le Demi-Monde* or *Les Idées de Madame Aubray.*

Nor is *Michel Pauper* free from the influence of melodrama which had become so popular during the nineteenth century. Especially noteworthy is the scene in which Hélène, on her wedding night, leaving the house with the Count, steps over the body of her drunken husband lying in their path, or the scene in which Michel, after destroying the crystal block in his delirium, falls dead, his head surrounded by a shower of diamonds.

Michel Pauper is, then, a sort of potpourri in which Becque, at the crossroads of his career, introduced all the diverse tendencies of his day. Stylistically, it has nothing in common with *Les Corbeaux* or *La Parisienne.* Rhetorical, even grandiloquent, stilted and pompous, it often verges on the ludicrous. Madame de la Roseraye's monologue in Act II ("Oh men, men! how frivolous, ungrateful, and cruel you are! You choose the most noble creatures for your victims and you brush them aside without pity, after striking them without remorse!") or the equally sentimental speech of Hélène in the same act ("Come, come, my nobleman, my warrior; in seeing you I forget all the tears that you cost me. Come quickly that I may admire your proud haughty figure . . . bring into my prison words of liberty, songs of revolt!") are among the unbelievably stilted passages that abound throughout the entire five acts.

Becque also shows a fondness for sententious expression ("The bottle is sometimes a worse mistress than the others") or for pompous phrases ("Madame de la Roseraye teaches me respect for her virtues"). Small wonder that, when the play was revived in 1872 and again in 1886, Becque attempted, with only partial success, to reduce the preaching and to tone down the declamatory style.

In its construction *Michel Pauper* likewise leaves much to be desired. The principal theme–that of rehabilitation though love–is essentially a romantic one, and Becque has failed to integrate it successfully with his treatment of the social questions which he briefly introduces. The scene in which Michel is surrounded by admiring workers who come to express their gratitude seems out of place and out of key with the rest of the play, while that in which the Baron Von-Der-Holweck lectures his cousin on his moral conduct serves no real function from the standpoint of dramatic action and might just as well have been omitted.

Like the dramas of Victor Hugo, *Michel Pauper* is built on antithesis of situation and of character. Throughout the play Becque contrasts inherited greatness with acquired greatness and opposes the humble workman to the corrupt nobility. Like Hugo, also, he fails to motivate his characters satisfactorily. Michel's sudden transformation from a drunken workman to an inventor of genius and a paragon of virtue strains the credulity of the reader as much as does the transformation of Ruy Blas from a simple valet to a great statesman. His return to drunkenness after his disillusionment, though more plausible from the psychological standpoint, seems equally melodramatic.

Hélène, madly in love with the arrogant, dominating, and ruthless Count, is hardly more convincing than Michel or the Count himself and at times dimly recalls the Mathilde of *Le Rouge et le Noir.* Among the tinsel characters, only Monsieur de la Roseraye seems to be alive, but his role is only a minor one and mainly serves as a point of departure for the rest of the play. Madame de la Roseraye prefigures Madame Vigneron of *Les Corbeaux,* but is more stereotyped and colorless; the Baron seems to have no other function than that of a *raisonneur.* Both are almost painfully virtuous and indulge in long moral disquisitions that become monotonous and irritating.

In later years Becque must have recognized the weakness of his drama with its strange mixture of Romanticism, Realism, and melodrama, and it is perhaps for this reason that he makes only a passing reference to the play in his *Souvenirs d'un auteur dramatique.* The Becque of *Les Corbeaux* will reject the prolixity, the rhetoric, and the didacticism of *Michel Pauper* and will retain only its power, its pessimism, and its concern for the humble and the downtrodden.

CHAPTER 3

Three Minor Plays

I L'Enlèvement (The Elopement)

WITH the outbreak of the Franco-Prussian War, Becque enlisted as a simple soldier and took part in the siege of Paris. A man of deep patriotism, he never failed to put love of country before all else, even before his love for the theater. "For a good military law which would satisfy the country and guarantee its security, one would give all the *Chéries* [Edmond de Goncourt] on earth, all the *Boules de suif* [Maupassant], all the Corbeaux" (V, 132), he was to write many years later, in an article attacking the indifference of contemporary writers to political and governmental matters.

Becque's stay in the army, however, did nothing to diminish his interest in the theater or to lessen his desire to become a successful dramatist. In the period of gloom that followed the invasion, he started work on a new drama, *L'Enlèvement,* working hastily–too hastily, as he later admitted–in order to satisfy his pressing need for money. Presented at the Vaudeville on November 18, 1871, *L'Enlèvement* proved to be, in the author's words, "a brilliant failure" (II, 337). Five nights later, he explains in the preface to the play, it was withdrawn after being "hissed and booed the first evening and annihilated by critics the next" (IV, I). Becque was not overstating the case. Except for a few solitary voices raised in his defense, the critics were mainly hostile. One of them, Auguste Vitu, went so far as to suggest that the unhappy author quit the theater for good (I, 22). Even Becque's grandnephew and editor, Jean Robaglia, was to agree many years later that *L'Enlèvement* was unsuited for dramatic production (I, 22).

Becque made no attempt to publish the play until twenty-five years later when it appeared in the *Revue du Palais* on May 1, 1897, preceded by a short preface in which the crestfallen author wrote somewhat apologetically: "I shall not complain if it is found mediocre. If any part of it, however, should not be without merit, I would be pleased to have it pointed out to me. It would be the first time" (IV, II).

Three Minor Plays

Despite Becque's intense dislike for the thesis play and his claim, made many years later, that he had "never dreamed of rehashing those two stale themes of dramatic art: divorce and illegitimacy" (II, 339), *L'Enlèvement* is itself a thesis play in favor of divorce. When Becque wrote his drama in 1871, however, the subject was still a novel one. It is true that Dumas *fils* had been pleading the cause of divorce in the salons of the day, but it was not until 1876 that he published his drama *L'Etrangère (The Foreigner)* in which he attempted to prove the need for reestablishing the divorce law that had been suppressed in 1816. It was also in 1876 that Augier argued a similar thesis in his play *Madame Caverlet.* In fact, the subject continued to be exploited by playwrights even after 1884 when, on July 27, the divorce law was finally reenacted.

The fact that Becque may have aroused the hostility of a conservative public by treating so provocative a subject for the first time could explain to some extent the resounding failure of the play. *L'Enlèvement* is hardly so inferior to *Michel Pauper* that it deserves the condemnation with which it met. Later critics, however, were more tolerant in their judgment. Edmond Sée considers *L'Enlèvement* the best of Becque's early plays and the one which offers the clearest indication of his genius.[1] Huneker likewise feels that Becque handled the problem of divorce with consummate skill and that, in concealing the technical processes of the drama, he revealed great art even while giving the impression of being completely artless.[2]

It seems difficult, however, to justify their praise and to admire to the same extent the psychological penetration and economy of action to which they point. The drama lacks all the power of *Michel Pauper* while retaining its verbose and declamatory style. If *L'Enlèvement* proved unsuccessful, it is chiefly because Becque failed to translate ideas and emotions into dramatic action and instead relied too heavily on interminable discussions as a means of convincing the spectator. Where a play like *La Parisienne* begins in medias res with the exposition already a part of the action, *L'Enlèvement* begins with several long *récits* which explain to the audience all that the protagonists have experienced up to that point. The reader learns that Emma de Sainte-Croix is an admirable and intelligent woman who has been deceived and neglected by her husband Raoul ever since her marriage. Emma loves and in turn is loved by Monsieur de la Rouve, who is equally admirable and who has also been deceived and disappointed in marriage.

The play proceeds in the form of arguments for and against Emma's elopement with de la Rouve. The elder Madame de Sainte-Croix, though sympathetic in the face of Emma's unhappiness, tries to convince her daughter-in-law that separation will expose her to public scorn and only increase her unhappiness and misery; Monsieur de la Rouve counters her argument by insisting that fidelity to an unworthy husband is in itself a wrong and that Emma is unnecessarily a victim of an unjust system.

Won over by the arguments of her mother-in-law, Emma agrees to a trial reconciliation with Raoul. In the meantime, Antoinette, the mistress of Emma's husband, arrives unexpectedly under the assumed name of the Countess Bordogni. The absurd behavior of Antoinette, acting what she believes to be the role of a woman in high society, transforms the play from social drama into farce. But with the sudden discovery that Antoinette is the ignoble wife of de la Rouve, *L'Enlèvement* turns from farce to melodrama, and Emma, in a highly theatrical final scene, renounces her attempt at a reconciliation and leaves to become the mistress of her admirer.

The dialogue, like that of *Michel Pauper,* is more often than not stilted and grandiloquent. Emma's long monologue (a full page and a half), in which she bemoans the lot of women in the social system and berates her husband and mother-in-law, is too declamatory to be either moving or convincing:

Vulgar woman, speaker of idle and commonplace remarks, yes, you are indeed your son's mother, and you are even superior to him! At least your life does not lack harmony; it has the grandeur of regular patterns. You have been honest, devoted, kind; you have also been frivolous and narrow-minded. That is the lot of women, apparently, and you have accepted it. But your wretched son, that worthless and maleficent man, blessed to the point of injustice with the favors of this world, only makes further demands on the world! (Act III, sc. 5)

She continues in what seems almost a mock Corneillian manner:

Honor, duty, respect, I have revered those great words as much as anyone, and I would have liked to display a free mind obedient to accepted rules. My husband did not permit it. In my eyes he is no more than a neutral banner to be used as a cover or to be discarded.

De la Rouve's attack on the divorce law is even more rhetorical and self-conscious:

Down with that miserable law that forever cements an impossible union and pits against each other two people whom it has joined together!

Down with that miserable law which has no punishment for the deserter and which abandons the flag-bearer! Down with that miserable law which, by elevating a social rule above divine decrees, thrusts you today, Madame, after your heroic isolation, into a monstrous reconcilation! (Act I, sc. 1)

Throughout the play Becque tends to indulge in a pompous labored style that wearies the reader and often taxes his patience: "Withdraw, Madame, this creature besmirches all that with which she comes in contact" (Act II, sc. 8); "The splatter falls back into the stream from which it came" (Act II, sc. 9). In addition to Antoinette, only Raoul is free from the turgid prose that marks so much of the play, in part because he is not obliged to share in presenting the thesis and more especially because in his role of dandy and rake he is assigned the cynical witticisms for which Becque was so well known in real life.

The characters are as mannered and pompous as their language. Emma is too cerebral, too much the bluestocking to be completely sympathetic, de la Rouve too self-righteous, too given to solemn preachments. Madame de Sainte-Croix thinks only of her son and of preserving the marriage which she had encouraged. All three characters exist only to represent the various aspects of the problem and to express the author's ideas about that problem. If Raoul and Antoinette seem less wooden than the others, they are, on the other hand, more exaggerated and too close to the stock characters of farce and melodrama.

As in the case of *Michel Pauper* and *L'Enfant prodigue, L'Enlèvement* offers little reason to suspect that some years later its author would produce one of the dramatic masterpieces of the century. But Becque was astute enough to recognize his faults, and that knowledge, added to his instinct as a dramatist, was to allow him to overcome his weaknesses and to cultivate those qualities which, though scarcely evident in his early plays, were to transform the tired drama of his day into something vigorous and new.

II La Navette (The Shuttle)

After the failure of *L'Enlèvement,* Becque was left at loose ends. Though he was nearing forty, he had yet to establish himself or to attain any sort of financial security. To earn a living he was forced to take a job first at the office of the Legion of Honor and then at the Stock Exchange. But despite his mediocre success in the theater, he was unwilling to give up his dream of becoming a great dramatist, and around 1872 or 1873–certainly no later than 1876–he set to work on a play which he hoped would give proof of his ability. The result was *Les Corbeaux.*

Although the play was later acclaimed a masterpiece, Becque could find no theater willing to undertake a work so unconventional, so lacking in all the standard ingredients of the "well-made play." Deeply disappointed, he decided to return to the genre which had first brought him success. "I had submitted *Les Corbeaux* everywhere, and everywhere it had been refused. I clearly wasn't in a mood to begin another important work. I didn't quite know what to do; I wrote *La Navette"* (III, 181).

Perhaps the bitterness of his disappointment explains to some extent the more mordant tone, so unlike that of *L'Enfant prodigue.* A clever and amusing comedy in one act, *La Navette* is deeply ironic in its rigorous observation of the foibles and egoistic character of its protagonists. Even more clearly than *L'Enfant prodigue,* it reveals Becque's tendency to move toward a comedy of manners and character. Plot has become strictly secondary, or, more properly speaking, intrigue has been reduced to the presentation of a comic situation which allows the author to exploit to the fullest the behavior of his characters.

Like many of the plays of the day, *La Navette* is concerned with the demimonde and has as its protagonist a courtesan. But, unlike his contemporaries, Becque makes no attempt either to sentimentalize or to condemn. Antonia is neither a Marguerite Gautier, rehabilitated and ennobled by love, nor a Suzanne d'Ange, scheming to obtain a place in respectable society. Antonia, on the contrary, is perfectly content in her role. As incapable of deep feeling as she is of cruelty or viciousness, she has enough common sense to look out for her own interests and enough capriciousness and coquetry to enjoy the excitement of an affair on the side.

Antonia is kept by Alfred, a serious young man, self-centered, frugal, and gravely concerned with preserving his dignity. Reminded constantly by his mistress that he had failed to secure the life annuity which he had promised her, Alfred begins to look back nostalgically to the days when Antonia had had a rich protector, and he had enjoyed her favors in secret without having to assume any financial responsibilities. He even regrets having insisted, out of a sense of dignity, that Antonia dismiss her protector and devote herself exclusively to him.

Alfred is unaware that Antonia has secretly been entertaining another young man, Arthur, who, like Alfred before him, finds it degrading to be competing for the favors of his mistress. At Arthur's request, Antonia dismisses Alfred. Arthur now finds himself in the same position as Alfred, and, like his predecessor, he assumes the same role of protector and moral adviser. As bored by the changed Arthur as she had been by Alfred, Antonia secretly accepts the attention of another young admirer, Armand. But Arthur soon finds his financial obligations little to his liking and longs for the days when he was free to enjoy love at another's expense. At Arthur's suggestion, Antonia agrees to revert to the previous arrangement and to take back Alfred who returns, repentant and willing to submit to all her demands.

Slight as it is, the play is not without interest. Gone is the rhetoric of the earlier dramas; in its stead there is an economy of action and of words which anticipates *La Parisienne.* In fact, *La Navette* is in many ways an early version of Becque's ironic masterpiece. The comic element results from certain mechanical effects which Becque deliberately sought and exploited. Not only does the situation repeat itself so that the play ends just as it had begun, but even the characters are given a mechanical sameness. By giving each of the three men a name beginning with the same letter and containing the same number of letters, Becque has further emphasized the mechanical aspect of their roles.

There is no essential difference between Alfred and Arthur either in their outlook or in their reaction to the situation at hand. Both are completely average and commonplace in intelligence, character, and personality. Both are selfish, vain, and almost pathetically concerned with the wish to dignify their situation, to maintain appearances, and to make Antonia into something better than she is. Arthur, who had formerly brought Antonia a copy of *L'Assommoir (The Dram Shop),* cautions her that he will no longer permit her to read Zola and that henceforth he will take her to the Comédie-Française or to the Opéra Comique rather than to the Variétés. Like Alfred, he advises her to seek a reconciliation with her mother. "There is no better company for a woman than the society of her mother," he gravely remarks.

Antonia is equally commonplace and lacking in dramatic qualities. Not one to be swept off her feet by passion or deep emotion, she retains all the practicality of a good bourgeoise, while safely indulging any whim that will make life less boring and monotonous. Like Clotilde of *La Parisienne,* she is completely devoid of conscience and quite obtuse about her changes of heart. When she decides to replace Alfred, who had become more serious and less carefree with his responsibilities, she remarks with delightful inconsequence: "I was crazy about that fellow and now I can hardly stand to look at him. How men change!" When she has to keep Armand waiting while she gets rid of Arthur, she insists that he play a game of bezique, just as she had done on earlier occasions with Alfred and then in turn with Arthur. The merry-go-round never stops; the characters simply change places.

It is not strange that *La Navette* left its spectators strangely ill at ease. Accustomed to the moralizing that usually accompanied the dramatic enactment of human weakness, they were baffled by the author's cold impersonality and by his failure to comment on the antics of his characters. Perhaps, too, they were conscious of his contempt for people not too unlike themselves and unwilling to admit that that very contempt was in itself a moral commentary more powerful than the sugarcoated preachments to which they were accustomed.

Whatever the case, Becque found that almost none of the theaters wished to take the risk of presenting *La Navette.* After having made his usual canvass of the theaters, he finally succeeded in placing it at the Gymnase where it opened on November 15, 1878, despite the objections of most of the theatrical staff. The comedy ran for only three weeks, and, although it contained not a single prurient line nor the slightest action that could be considered suggestive, it was severely criticized by most reviewers, who saw in it only another example of "la littérature putride" associated with Zola and his followers.

Surprisingly enough, Sarcey was one of the few who recognized the originality of treatment, the spontaneity of dialogue, and the power of observation that distinguished what to him was otherwise a mere vaudeville, somewhat crude in its choice of subject. A few years later, the genuine merit of *La Navette* was more widely acknowledged, and critics from Anatole France in 1890 to Robert de Flers in 1914 did not hesitate to praise the dramatic skill that Becque had revealed both in the conception and execution of his delightful one-act comedy.

III Les Honnêtes Femmes (The Respectable Women)

Unwilling to accept defeat, Becque composed still another curtain raiser, *Les Honnêtes Femmes,* which he is said to have written in one night after mulling it over in his mind for some weeks beforehand. Presented on January 1, 1880 at the Gymnase, it caused little stir–so little, in fact, that none of the important journals of the day even bothered to mention it. Five years later it was performed with considerable success at the Renaissance, where it served as a companion piece for *La Parisienne,* and on October 27, 1886 it was revived by the Comédie-Française, where it had a run of twenty performances.

In his *Souvenirs* Becque admits that *Les Honnêtes Femmes* enjoyed a greater success than it deserved and adds that it was only the second work to bring him any money. Becque was certainly not overestimating the play, and one wonders why he would have bothered to write anything so flat and banal. It may well be that he wished to show the public that he was capable of treating virtuous as well as morally weak characters and that he was far from belonging to the Naturalistic school, for which he had only the greatest contempt.

In contrast to Antonia, Madame Chevalier and Geneviève, the daughter of a dear friend, are completely honorable and admirable. Lambert, attracted by the serene charm of Madame Chevalier, tries to persuade her to become his mistress. Uninterested in his offer, Madame Chevalier leads him on, thinking he might be a good match for Geneviève, who happens to be paying her a visit. Lambert, deceived by Madame Chevalier's interest in his age and financial status, begins to wonder if she is really "respectable" and feels quite convinced that he has made a conquest. It is only then that she tries to persuade him to marry and settle down and that she proposes Geneviève as an ideal wife who will bring him the happiness he desires.

The play is so skillfully structured that no exposition is required to provide the audience with an explanation of the situation at hand. No more than three characters are involved, if the maid, whose role is minimal, is excluded, and of these three only Madame Chevalier and Lambert have any dramatic importance. Like some of the plays of Musset, plot is reduced to a conversation between two people—a conversation in which the poetic charm and the exquisite grace of the Romantic poet are replaced by the natural and animated dialogue of everyday people in an everyday world. The cynicism of *La Navette* is supplanted by a quiet serenity and by the solid values of the bourgeois world which Becque so greatly admired in his mother and sister. But neither the structure nor the characterization are sufficiently strong to justify its success, and without the biting wit which he handles so well and which the subject precludes, the play verges on the saccharine. One can only agree with Becque that the success of *Les Honnêtes Femmes* exceeded its real merit.

CHAPTER 4

Les Corbeaux (The Vultures)

I *Date of Composition and Opening Night*

THE complete indifference with which *Les Honnêtes Femmes* had been received only added to Becque's discouragement and further dampened his hopes of having *Les Corbeaux* performed on the French stage. Refusing to compromise or to make the changes demanded by hesitant directors, he decided to accept defeat and content himself with its publication.

It was then that Stock, his publisher who had already sent the manuscript to the printer, discovered that Becque had felt it useless to approach the Comédie-Française in his search for a producer. At Stock's suggestion, the corrected manuscript was submitted to Thierry, director of the Arsenal Library and former administrator of the Comédie.[1] Impressed by the power and originality of the play, Thierry recommended it to Perrin, his successor at the Comédie. Perrin followed Thierry's recommendation, and, on September 14, 1882, *Les Corbeaux* was presented at the Comédie-Française before a large and curious audience. All of his life Becque remained deeply grateful to Thierry for his support and never failed to insist that it was Thierry rather than Perrin or Lacroix, the reader at the Comédie, who was responsible for discovering his drama (VI, 19).

The time that had elapsed between the writing of *Les Corbeaux* and its production had been long and disheartening. Until 1924 it was generally assumed that Becque had written the play in 1876, since he himself speaks of a period of five years in which he tried to get the play accepted. If those five years, in addition to the year spent in writing, are counted back from 1882, the date would indeed be 1876. If, however, as Emile Bouvier believes, the five years date back from 1878 when, in desperation, Becque put aside *Les Corbeaux* and wrote *La Navette,* the play would have been written as early as 1872, and Becque's boldness and independence in breaking with traditional drama would be even more remarkable.[2] The problem is almost insoluble, since plausible arguments can be found for and against both theories.

The play was put in rehearsal and Becque who, as usual, insisted on coaching the actors, proved no easy taskmaster. His determination that his wishes be followed in every detail irritated and exasperated the actors who were already disturbed by the unconventional nature of the play. Becque had no hesitations about his interpretation. After all, he had spent an entire year writing and rewriting *Les Corbeaux.* Pacing back and forth in his apartment on the rue Matignon, he had sought the exact phrase, the right accent, while watching every movement in the mirror. At other times, walking along the Champs-Elysées in the early morning hours, gesticulating and talking to himself, he had created some of his finest dialogue.

Despite the dissatisfaction of the actors, Becque succeeded in having his way until the night of the final dress rehearsal when the audience, accustomed to the technique of the "well-made play," showed their shock and dismay at his departure from the norm. His failure to end the play after Marie's betrothal to Teissier, the scene between Blanche and the heartless Madame de Saint-Genis, and the scene in which Gaston impersonates his father shortly before the unexpected death of the latter, all met with sharp criticism. Word spread that the play would be a failure, and Perrin and the actors, with Coquelin as their leader, insisted that Becque make certain concessions. Persuaded of the risks he was running, the anxious author finally yielded, and the play was given without the last two scenes and without Gaston's harmless impersonation. Less radical changes included eliminating a few colloquial expressions and shortening the scene in which Madame Vigneron is completely outwitted and duped by her husband's lawyer, Monsieur Bourdon.

The opening night proved to be a success in spite of certain tense moments. The first act met with restrained approval; the second received a mixed reception, although the scene of consultation among the four women was warmly applauded. The controversial scene between Blanche and Madame de Saint-Genis aroused intense disapproval, and, at one point, the audience hissed so loudly that the actress who played the role of the older woman fled the stage without giving the cue for the final important words of Blanche. With admirable presence of mind, Mademoiselle Reichemberg, who played the part of Blanche, continued as if nothing had happened and spoke her last lines with such simple and moving poignancy that the audience, completely won over, gave her an ovation. The fourth and final act was received more or less quietly. There was no longer any doubt. Becque had finally scored a victory.

II *Theme*

In spite of its initial success, *Les Corbeaux* had little appeal for the general public and was given only eighteen performances. Immensely superior in technique and in dramatic power to *Michel Pauper* and to *L'Enlèvement,* it reveals the same interest in social injustice and the same deep humanitarian concern. Becque himself has explained the purpose of his play: "I had been struck many times by the dangers that a family runs and by the ruin into which it often falls after the death of the husband and father" (II, 338).

It is just such a situation that Becque portrays in his moving drama. On the sudden death of Monsieur Vigneron, a wealthy manufacturer, Madame Vigneron, her three daughters, and a worthless son are left prey to a dishonest partner and to an unprincipled notary by whom they are stripped of their heritage. Disaster follows upon disaster. Gaston, the irresponsible young son, abandons the family and enlists in the army. Blanche, whose approaching marriage to a young impoverished aristocrat is broken off by the calculating mother of her fiancé, loses her mind and becomes an added burden. The home and fortune of the family are lost forever. In a desperate effort to save the family from abject poverty and ruin, Marie, the second daughter, is forced to marry her father's former partner, Monsieur Teissier, a sixty-year-old Harpagon who takes advantage of the very misfortune which he has brought upon his victims.

Though the play is concerned with the problem of social justice, Becque is careful to avoid the pitfalls of a thesis play and to present only what he calls "a general observation" of a real-life situation. "It was a thesis, if you insist. It was rather a general observation, very simple and very clear, which could be framed within a play without harming the truth of the characters" (II, 338). Nor does Becque resort to the use of a *raisonneur* as he had done in *Michel Pauper.* The ideas, implicit rather than explicit, are presented indirectly through the action of the characters. No better example could be found of what he was to affirm in his lecture on Dumas *fils* in 1895: "The serious element of the theater is not in the ideas. It is in the digestion of the ideas by the characters, in the dramatic or comic force which the characters give to the ideas" (VII, 76).

The theme of the play becomes obvious to the spectator long before Rosalie, the faithful servant, sums up the situation to Merckens, the music teacher, who sees the poverty of the new lodgings for the first time: "The poor lady and her young girls are ruined, my dear Sir, ruined! I shan't tell you how it happened, but I can't get the idea out of my head. You see, when businessmen arrive after a death, you might as well say: here come the vultures! They only leave what they can't carry away" (Act IV, scene 1).

Although *Les Corbeaux* is often criticized for its pessimistic outlook on life, it clearly reveals a deep pity and warm affection for the innocent, the weak and the helpless, which belie the pessimism and indicate a streak of idealism on the part of the author. "There is in me a sentimental revolutionary," Becque wrote in his preface to the play. "I have never had much taste for assassins, for the emotionally unstable, for alcoholics, for the martyrs of heredity and the victims of evolution. . . . But I love the innocent, the destitute, the heavily burdened, those who struggle against force and any form of tyranny" (II, 339).

Les Corbeaux is proof of his contention, for it is as much a defense of the weak and innocent as it is an attack on evil and injustice. Inspired by pity and love, Becque draws his portraits of the mother and three daughters with tenderness and skill. If he stresses the base villainy of the vultures, it is chiefly to arouse our pity for their victims. Our dislike for Madame de Saint-Genis–so intense that it unnerved the actress the opening night–is transformed into pity and sympathy of even greater intensity for her victim. Throughout the entire play, sympathy for the victims is being constantly generated by hatred of the oppressors. The one does not exist without the other. It is for this reason that Edmond Sée described the play as a "poem of grief, of pity" and that, despite their objections to Becque's dramatic system, several critics found themselves deeply moved by the tragic plight of the four women caught in a trap from which they could not extricate themselves.[3]

When the vultures have completed their devastation and the Vigneron family is saved from abject misery through the sacrifice of Marie, the spectator is left not so much with a feeling of anger as with a sense of deep pity and sadness. The ferocity of Becque's hatred for the oppressor gives way to his love for the oppressed, and the entire play assumes a tragic tone that is incompatible with the *comédie rosse* to which it is sometimes said to belong.

III *Idealism versus Pessimism*

Becque's pessimism is relieved not only by his pity and love for the weak and helpless; it is also mitigated by his belief in goodness and virtue. The members of the Vigneron family are evidence of this belief. In the first act, Monsieur Vigneron is shown as a loving husband and father and as a loyal and honest associate of his partner Teissier. Naïve and typically bourgeois in matters of culture, he has shown astute intelligence in business and has gained for himself the respect of his more shrewd and calculating associates. Despite the small fortune which he has attained through hard work and sacrifice, he has remained entirely unspoiled by success and attaches little importance to the wealth or position of others. The fact that Blanche is marrying into the upper class is a matter of indifference to him. In his eyes, his daughter's happiness is far more important than the social status of her fiancé. In fact, Vigneron shows a healthy scorn for the foppish appearance and manners of the man she has chosen to marry.

Madame Vigneron, less intelligent and even more naïve than her husband, lives only for her husband and children and is deeply concerned with their happiness and welfare. Though she frankly admits being flattered by the fact that her daughter is marrying a member of the nobility, she quickly adds: "But I wouldn't sacrifice the happiness of my daughter for any silly nonsense" (Act I, sc. 1). Her motherly lecture to her daughter is touching in its sincerity, and her reaction to Madame de Saint-Genis' schemes for making the young couple heirs to Teissier's fortune contrasts sharply with the calculating nature of the former.

The three Vigneron daughters share the same high principles and moral standards of their parents. Becque himself was keenly aware of the difference between his heroines and those of his contemporaries. When *Les Corbeaux* was revived in 1897, he is said to have remarked: "They are going to find me very old-fashioned; all my women are honorable" (I, 55). To be sure, more than twenty years had elapsed since the writing of the play, yet as late as 1890 Becque had evidently not changed his ideas. "I have always thought that *Les Corbeaux* was my best work," he wrote to Octave Mirbeau, "and to be perfectly honest, that my young girls were genuine young girls, that they represented the average young girl better than the detailed specimens drawn by my more illustrious colleagues" (VII, 219). Two years earlier he had written to the Belgian writer, Georges Rodenbach, that the writers of the *comédie rosse* were too prone to use only mediocre characters and lower-class surroundings (VII, 222).

The actual portrayal of the three young girls belies Becque's "black pessimism" as much as his statements to Mirbeau and Rodenbach. Blanche, who had trustingly yielded to her love for Georges, her fiancé, is tortured by a sense of guilt which makes her insist on the marriage that Madame de Saint-Genis refuses to allow after discovering that the fatherless young girl has been left without a dowry: "Do you think that, if it were a matter of an ordinary engagement, I would humiliate myself to the point of calling him [Georges] back? I would break my heart rather than offer it to one who would scorn it and wouldn't be worthy of it. . . . You talk to me about the future; the future will have to take care of itself. I can only think of the past—a past which will make me blush with shame and sorrow" (Act III, sc. 4).

The loss of her reason is not the result of frustrated or hopeless passion but rather of an overpowering sense of guilt that dwarfs all other emotions, even love itself. The cruel words "fallen woman," with which Madame de Saint-Genis heartlessly taunts her, finally causes her to break and to withdraw into the darkened shadows of her consciousness.

Judith, the eldest daughter, despite her willingness to make sacrifices for her family, can find no means by which to help them. Forced out of her little dream world by her father's death, she surmounts her moral prejudices and considers adopting a theatrical career in accordance with the advice given her in happier days by Merckens, her music professor. When the cynical Merckens now ridicules her plan and she is left with no way to turn, she is still unwilling to let Marie sacrifice herself for her family by marrying Teissier: "above all think only of yourself. . . . We would be more than guilty, you understand, more than guilty in advising you to make the greatest sacrifice that a woman can make" (Act IV, sc. 3).

In Marie, the second daughter, Becque has created one of his most sympathetic and admirable characters. More intelligent and practical than either her sisters or her mother, she is the one on whom they rely for guidance and protection. The idea of deserting her family and of saving herself does not occur to her for a moment, much to the surprise of Teissier. Moreover, even in the struggle for survival, Marie refuses to compromise her principles. In spite of her need to conciliate Teissier, she does not hesitate to send him away when she understands that the proposition he is making her is far from honorable. When Teissier finally decides to request her hand in marriage, she has but one question to ask of his emissary: "I would like to know, Monsieur Bourdon—and I beg you to answer frankly—if Monsieur Teissier is an honorable man." And she quickly adds, seeing that Bourdon is far from understanding her scruples: "An honorable man means many things to a young girl" (Act IV, sc. 6). When she finally accepts the offer of marriage, it is only because Teissier agrees to support her family, because she realizes there is no other way of saving them from abject poverty. "You see this marriage is our salvation," she tells her mother. "I am ashamed to enter into it, but I would be guilty if I didn't do so" (Act IV, sc. 7).

Becque's idealism is revealed not only in his portrayal of the members of the Vigneron family but also in his depiction of their faithful old servant, Rosalie. It is Rosalie who, with her simple good sense, realizes almost instinctively the dishonesty of Monsieur Vigneron's associates and foresees the destruction that they will accomplish. And it is Rosalie who, with her loyalty and deep affection, stays with the family to the end, sharing their sorrow and misery and offering them the little comfort and protection that she can.

It has been suggested that Rosalie is based on the goodhearted servant of popular melodrama. Others claim that she was inspired by the comedies of Molière where the family servant so often plays an important role. Although she shows some of the sharp insight characteristic of Dorine in *Le Tartuffe,* she reveals none of her initiative and sly resourcefulness. In her simple devotion and loyalty she is more reminiscent of *Félicité* in Flaubert's *Un Coeur Simple (A Simple Heart)* or even of "la servante au grand coeur" in the poem of Baudelaire by that name.

Rosalie, like the members of the Vigneron family, clearly reveals Becque's admiration for the simple virtues in life. In fact, Becque may even be called an optimist in his belief that purity of heart remains indestructible even in the face of the most adverse circumstances. If Becque can be termed a pessimist, it is only because he knows that evil and injustice bring needless suffering and unhappiness and that the good are often the victims of the bad.

IV *Innovations in Technique*

The revolutionary nature of Becque's technique in *Les Corbeaux* has been exaggerated almost as much as the pessimistic aspect of his philosophy. Although he does not hesitate to abandon the complicated action, the witty dialogue, and the well-known formulas of the "well-made play," it is not quite exact to say that he is presenting a "slice of life." Even while rejecting the artificial conventions so dear to Dumas *fils* and Augier and while introducing certain important innovations, he continues to use the traditional elements of dramatic technique. Like his fellow realist Ibsen, he even relies occasionally on the monologue and the aside.

One of the most salutary innovations that Becque introduces in *Les Corbeaux*—one that also explains to a certain extent his lack of popular success—is his rejection of such timeworn themes as love and adultery. Like Balzac in the novel, he introduces into his play a theme closely related to the mores of the day—greed for money, for personal enrichment at any price. Like Balzac also, he is concerned with the ruthlessness of the business world and with the evils that arise when clever but unscrupulous lawyers and businessmen take advantage of those who are ignorant of the law. In explaining to Blanche their precarious situation, Marie states the theme in its general form: "Money must indeed be important, since so many misfortunes happen when it is lacking and since it inspires so many evil actions" (Act II, sc. 5). Later in the play, Rosalie makes the theme even more explicit when she compares Vigneron's associates to vultures who leave nothing behind them.

Since Becque's day, themes involving the dishonesty and cruelty of the business world seem much less startling and have been frequently used not only by his disciples but by later writers as well. If such plays as Lavedan's *L'Argent (Money)* or Mirbeau's *Les Affaires sont les affaires (Business is Business)* found more ready acceptance, it was mainly because Becque had successfully prepared the way. To the audience of 1882, however, the subject of *Les Corbeaux* was much less palatable. It is said that on the opening night the galleries were filled with notaries who, having heard that their profession was being maligned in the much talked of play, came to see for themselves the nature and extent of Becque's attack.

Other innovations of Becque seem less striking, though to the audience of his day they must have seemed radical departures from the accepted norm. "We have done away with marriage," Becque once said in summarizing his accomplishments and those of his contemporaries (VII, 81). Though the statement does not apply fully to *Les Corbeaux,* it is indeed true that the marriage of Marie and Teissier does not bring about the usual happy ending. On the contrary, it only adds to the tragic effect of the play. Moreover, Becque does not hesitate to forego the usual showy denouement with all or most of the principal characters on stage. Instead he ends the play with a brilliant stroke of irony in an otherwise quiet and simple scene. Teissier, once the chief vulture and now the protector of the family, simply turns to Marie, after dismissing a dishonest bill collector, and assures her with unconscious irony: "You are surrounded by scoundrels, my child, since the death of your father."

A striking innovation, which met even with the approval of his contemporaries and which has continued to arouse universal admiration ever since, is the *procédé* used by Becque at the end of Act II. Madame Vigneron and her three daughters, gathered in a sort of family council, are desperately seeking some solution to their predicament. In the midst of their discussion a servant enters bringing a number of letters addressed to Madame Vigneron. At the request of her mother, Marie opens and reads them, one after the other, to her silent and stunned listeners. Each is a demand for money by greedy, unscrupulous creditors. As Marie, amid the dead silence, reaches for a fourth letter and gets ready to read, Madame Vigneron bursts into tears, and the curtain falls while the daughters look at each other sadly in silent despair. The effect is to prolong the action, to emphasize the endless accumulation of financial problems facing the family, and to create a powerful effect of tragic impotence.

Even more striking and unusual is the justly famous mute scene of Act IV that may have been inspired by Diderot's ideas of pantomime on the stage. In the dining room of the cheap lodging to which they have been forced to move, Madame Vigneron and her three daughters enter and sit down at the table. Madame Vigneron has grown gray and visibly older; Blanche, pale and listless with the vacant expression of the deranged, is seated by Marie. Rosalie stands nearby drinking her cup of *café au lait.* The atmosphere is heavy with sadness. The silence is prolonged until it becomes unbearable. Suddenly, Madame Vigneron bursts into tears and exclaims: "Ah, my children, if your father could see us now!" All break into tears, and the scene ends–a heartrending tableau whose silence is far more eloquent than words. No better example could be found of Diderot's belief that movement and gestures can be more effective than words in portraying a simple action.

V *Traditional Elements of Technique*

Aside from its innovations and its freedom from traditional rules and conventions, *Les Corbeaux* is almost classic in its technique. Far from being a "slice of life," it seems rather to fit Becque's own definition of the drama: "a composition which has a beginning, a middle, and an end." Act I shows the skill of its author in preparing for what follows. All the ensuing action has its germ within that opening act; all the characters are lightly sketched with an economy of line and a firmness of touch that will only require further shading in the acts to follow. At the same time, the exposition is so skillfully blended with the action that one is scarcely aware of its real purpose. The Vigneron family is seen happily engaged in various activities, as preparations are being made for a dinner at which Blanche's engagement will be celebrated and the marriage contract signed. One sees Monsieur and Madame Vigneron adoring their children, yet capable of lecturing them gently but firmly when they feel it needed; Blanche, sensitive and oblivious to all but her love; Judith, dreamy and wrapped up in her world of music; Marie, thoughtful and serious, anxious about her father's health; Gaston, irresponsible and badly spoiled by his doting father.

Just as precisely sketched are the dinner guests who in the following acts will cause the ruination of the family: Madame de Saint-Genis, the domineering mother of Georges, shrewd and calculating; Merckens, the music teacher, cynically complimenting Judith on the musical talents which he will later deride; Bourdon, sly and crafty, operating on the fringe of the law; and finally Teissier, selfish and miserly, who, even before his appearance, is made the center of interest.

The characters are revealed not only through their own words and actions but also through the comments of others. Throughout the entire act frequent references to Teissier prepare the spectators for the important role he will play. The outspoken dislike of the daughters, for which they are soundly lectured; Madame de Saint-Genis' description ("He has the eyes of a fox and the mouth of a monkey") are all confirmed by Teissier's own remarks on his arrival. His insistence on keeping his hat so that he may be certain of finding it again is suggestive of the miser, while his comical concern for his health ("It's very cold outside and very warm in here; I'll keep standing a few minutes to accustom myself to the temperature of your room") looks ahead to the motivation that will explain much of his eagerness to marry Marie.

As a result of Becque's careful preparation, the reader is not only given the key to the character and personality of each of the protagonists, but he also finds the germs of all the action to come. Madame de Saint-Genis' anxious concern for Blanche's dowry, her interest in Teissier's fortune, and her domination of her son ("Georges has always been obedient to me until now, and I intend to keep guiding him after his marriage. . . . I always act for him") prepare us for the breakup in the marriage plans. Blanche's quick whisper to Georges that she had been scolded by her mother for her lack of reserve with her fiancé, and her admission ("I didn't know what she was going to say to me, I got worried") already suggest what will be made more explicit in her talk with Marie and Madame de Saint-Genis. Even the despoiling of Vigneron's fortune by his associates becomes perfectly logical and almost inevitable, given the character of the vultures and Vigneron's own explanation of his financial status. Before leaving the house to go to his office, despite his feeling of fatigue and vertigo, he explains: "If I did what I wanted, my dears, I'd put on my dressing gown again and I'd wait for dinner with you. Unfortunately, my work doesn't do itself and I don't have the income to live without working. That will come perhaps, when I am the owner. But I have to wait, first for my houses to be built and second for my children to be established" (Act I, sc. 1).

The announcement of the sudden death of Monsieur Vigneron, coming at the end of the first act and immediately after the scene in which Gaston does a good-natured impersonation of his father, has often been unjustly criticized as a *coup de théâtre.* It is unfair to maintain that Becque does not prepare us for his unexpected death. On the contrary, he seems to make a special effort to forewarn the reader. Throughout the entire act, numerous references are made to Vigneron's health. The anxious concern of his wife and daughter, his reluctance to see a doctor, his own admission that he felt tired and slightly dizzy after closing his inventory—all are suggested by Becque with deliberate intent. The spectators are left shocked by the announcement, but they are certainly not unprepared.

Moreover, it should be remembered that Vigneron's death is merely a point of departure, just as is the false announcement of the death of Thésée in Racine's *Phèdre.* Vigneron's death, like that of Thésée, is simply a means of setting the play in motion. The subject of *Les Corbeaux* is not the demise of Monsieur Vigneron but the slow ruination of his family as a result of his death.

After the announcement of Monsieur Vigneron's death, which brings Act I to a sudden and climactic end, the play moves slowly and inexorably to its catastrophic finish. The bareness and simplicity of the plot and the lack of exterior action only serve to emphasize the dreary, gray existence which faces the four helpless victims. Each act builds slowly to a climax and ends on a note of tragedy: the death of Monsieur Vigneron in the first act, the endless piling up of creditors' bills in the second act, the insanity of Blanche in the third act, and Marie's decision to sacrifice her own happiness by marrying Teissier in the last act.

It has sometimes been claimed that the denouement of *Les Corbeaux* is typical of the "slice-of-life" technique. "Nothing is concluded, but everything goes on in another way, as in life," Edmond Sée has remarked in his study of Becque.[4] Others—both before and after Sée—have made the same observation.

Again the claim seems hardly justified in the light of the drama. The subject of the play is not the happiness of Marie and her family but rather their attempt to survive by escaping the clutches of their ruthless predators. If the problem of the drama is their struggle to survive, after being deprived of their protector, then that problem is indeed solved with the marriage of Marie, especially since the marriage agreement is based on Teissier's promise to provide for the entire family. That the solution is a tragic one for Marie has little or no bearing on the case. The particular problem–that of survival–has been solved and in a way that was not too uncommon in nineteenth-century France.

VI *Character Portrayal*

True to his own preaching, Becque depends less on action for his dramatic effect than on character portrayal and analysis. Both vultures and victims are portrayed with a power of observation and a psychological insight that make them live before our eyes. Moreover, no two characters are alike. Becque has endowed each one with a distinct personality that individualizes him and sets him apart from everyone else. In fact, it is often claimed that, since the Classicism of the seventeenth century, no drama has been so strictly a study of characters as *Les Corbeaux*.

Ever since Jules Lemaître and Emile Faguet pointed out the Classical tendencies in *Les Corbeaux* and compared the play to the comedies of Molière, critics have likened Teissier to Harpagon. A certain resemblance is inevitable, since both are misers and both are portrayed through the authors' emphasis on the comic fault. But where Harpagon is more obsessed with hiding his money box, Teissier is strictly a miser of the nineteenth century, quick to profit by any loopholes in the law and ready to take advantage of the weak and of those who are ignorant of their legal rights.

It seems a mistake to emphasize Teissier's sensuality, as is so often done. Only one of his remarks gives substance to the claim, a remark made by him when he first notices Marie's native intelligence in speaking of business matters: "Hardly twenty years old! But she is already a modest, sensible little person expressing herself very properly *(walking away)* and something her father didn't tell me: very appetizing (Act II, sc. 4).

Unlike Tartuffe, whose sensuality is as repulsive to the spectator as to Elvire, Teissier is less interested in Marie's physical charms than in her ability to do arithmetic. "Is she good at figures?" he keeps asking the various members of the household. Other remarks clearly show that Marie's attractiveness in his eyes is really a fringe benefit rather than the sole cause of his admiration. In fact, the reader is somewhat inclined to agree with Madame Vigneron who, on being asked by Madame de Saint-Genis if Teissier had a mistress, replies in great astonishment: "Monsieur Teissier, a mistress! For heaven's sake, what for?" (Act I, sc. 4).

That Teissier is concerned with finding someone to take care of him, someone whose intelligence, honesty, and common sense would be useful to him, is made clear in his questioning of Judith:

Teissier: Does she have a good reputation?
Judith: Very good.
Teissier: Simple tastes?
Judith: Very simple.
Teissier: Is she the sort of woman who would gladly stay home and take care of an older person?
Judith: Perhaps.
Teissier: Could one entrust the house keys to her without any worry? (Act III, sc. 2)

To Marie he explains frankly: "One doesn't complain about being alone as long as one is young; at my age it is a worry and a risk. . . . I would like very much to find a simple, sweet, and reliable young lady who would conduct herself decently in my house and not squander everything" (Act III, sc. 8).

And when Marie finally accepts his proposal of marriage, his old-fashioned gallantry gives little hint of sensuality and causes even Marie to smile. After kissing her on both cheeks, he explains in an almost fatherly manner: "Don't blush. This is the way one gets engaged in my home town. One kisses his fiancée, first on the right cheek, saying: That's for the mayor; then on the left cheek, saying: That's for the priest" (Act IV, sc. 8).

The last scene, in addition to its powerful irony, is further evidence of Teissier's motivation. Now that Marie has agreed to marry him, his first concern is to see how well she will be able to cope with the dishonesty of others. Leaving her alone with Dubois, the upholsterer, who had come to demand payment on a bill that had already been paid, he adds: "She will soon be the lady of the house. I'd like to see how she will act. . . . I'll be here behind the door, I shan't miss a word." His protective attitude to her when he decides to intervene–he who had been the most dangerous of the vultures–minimizes his sensuality and adds a bit of pungent irony to the denouement. "You are surrounded by scoundrels, my child, since the death of your father," he tells her solemnly as the curtain slowly falls. Unconscious irony could hardly be carried further.

Other characters in *Les Corbeaux* are presented with much the same dexterity, though with fewer details. Even minor characters are drawn with consummate skill and made to live before our eyes: Lefort with his vulgar, tactless manner, his willingness to oppose the other vultures until they agree to share their plunder with him; Dubois who, though threatening and overbearing with Marie, cringes before Teissier and hastily removes his hat, which he so rudely had worn in the presence of the young girl; Merckens, servile and flattering when he believes Judith to be an heiress, indifferent and almost insolent when he sees that there is nothing more for him to gain.

The characters of *Les Corbeaux* are made even more true to life by Becque's skillful use of dialogue. All speak the language of the day–idiomatic, familiar, and even slangy–with none of the artificiality that marked most of the contemporary drama. His ability to find the expression most suited to each character produces an extremely natural effect and leaves the impression of a conversation overheard in real life.

Moreover, like Molière, Becque has the remarkable ability to find a phrase that epitomizes the whole character and personality of his protagonists. Madame de Saint-Genis' "Don't trust anyone" and Teissier's "Is she good at figures?" are as eloquent and unforgettable as Harpagon's "without a dowry" or Orgon's "the poor man." Madame Vigneron's naïveté and helplessness are clearly revealed in her stubbornly repeated "As long as I am alive, the factory will not be sold," while Teissier's selfishness shows itself in his surprised discovery that Marie was making a purse intended for a sale to benefit the poor: "For the poor? You mean you are working for them while they do nothing?"

It has often been said that the victims are entirely passive, that they yield without a struggle and make no effort to stave off disaster. It is the futility of their feeble attempts, the one-sided aspect of the struggle that gives this impression of passivity. In her encounter with Madame de Saint-Genis, Blanche, surprisingly enough, shows unexpected will power and courage. No longer a young girl, she is suddenly a woman, capable of retaliation and even of threatening blackmail, when she finds that George's mother is adamant: "If I am dealing with a coward, who hides behind his mother's back, he had better not abandon me so casually. Wherever he goes, I will find him. I'll destroy his position and ruin his future" (Act III, sc. 9). If she confesses her fault in a last desperate effort to sway Madame de Saint-Genis, it is because it is the only weapon with which she can fight. But unfortunately, that weapon is of no avail.

Judith, more passive than either of her two sisters, seems less willing or able to struggle. But even Judith had hoped to support her family by adopting a musical career. When, after her discussion with Merckens, she sees the impossibility of her project, she can only say to Marie: "It seems to me that it is I, your oldest sister, your big sister as you call me, who ought to get us out of this trouble and get the family back on its feet. How? I haven't the least idea. I look for ways and don't find any. If it were only a matter of throwing myself in the fire, I would have done so already" (Act IV, sc. 3).

Madame Vigneron is no less helpless, and her attempts to save the family fortune are equally futile. At one moment she naïvely decides to replace the sly Bourdon by a notary whose card she had received in the mail, but her decision is quickly dissolved when she learns that the man in question had been convicted of fraud. Though she stubbornly repeats, with no understanding of the situation, that no one will touch the factory as long as she is alive, her determination is quickly and ironically broken, and she sinks weeping upon the *canapé*: "Leave me alone with your law. If I had to spend many days like this, my children, my strength would give out; you would have neither father nor mother before very long" (Act II, sc. 9).

Marie's will is less easily broken, but her desperate and frail efforts, like those of her mother and sisters, are of no more avail than the frantic beat of insect wings against a thick window pane. She discovers what Merckens had already so cynically told her sister Judith: "There is no recourse for a woman, or rather there is only one" (Act IV, sc. 2). To save her family she is forced to sacrifice her own happiness by selling herself in marriage to the most avaricious of their creditors.

In depicting the one-sided struggle of victims pitted against oppressors, Becque has succeeded in arousing emotions of deep pity on the part of the spectator. At the same time, there is a certain dignity and restraint about the tragic situation which results in part from the simplicity of the means employed. No wild, inarticulate cries, no hysterical outbursts occur as in the more melodramatic plays of a Bernstein or a Sardou. When Marie, left alone on the stage after her first encounter with Teissier, bursts into tears and sobs "my father, my father," the poignancy of the situation is in direct relation to the moving simplicity of the scene.

Marie's decision to accept Teissier's proposal is equally moving, and quietly dramatic. It is her love not only for her family but also for her dead father that motivates her decision and leaves her no more room for hesitation. At the beginning of the scene, she is clearly uncertain until Bourdon speaks to her in the name of her father: "He [Monsieur Vigneron] knew life; he knew that everything is paid for in this world; and, in the final analysis, his thought would be this today: I lived for my family, I died for them; my daughter can certainly sacrifice a few years for them" (Act IV, sc. 6).

It is at this moment that, disregarding her mother's request to speak to her in private, she answers Bourdon quietly, her eyes filled with tears: "Tell Monsieur Teissier that I accept." Then turning to her mother, as the notary leaves the room, she adds with moving pathos: "Kiss me, but don't say anything. Don't rob me of my courage. I haven't any more than I need. Bourdon is right; you see this marriage is our salvation. I am ashamed to enter into it and I would be guilty not to do so." The problem of survival has been solved but only at the expense of Marie's happiness and self-respect.

VII Les Corbeaux *and the Critics*

Critical reaction to *Les Corbeaux* was intense and often contradictory. Many who found the play grimly depressing accused Becque of adopting the brutality and the cynicism of the Naturalistic school. Sarcey at first joined the detractors and reproached Becque for depicting only the moral ugliness of life, though in later reviews he modified his judgment considerably and agreed that the play, remarkable in many ways, showed great promise on the part of the author.

Other critics, opposed to the artificiality of the "well-made play" and favoring the Naturalistic movement, were wildly enthusiastic in their praise and admired the very things that were being condemned by many of their colleagues. Henry Bauër was so deeply impressed that early the next morning he climbed the five flights to Becque's apartment to tell him that he considered *Les Corbeaux* a great masterpiece. From their meeting that day there developed a friendship that was to last all of Becque's life. Strangely enough, the leaders of the Naturalistic school were silent. Zola, who was later to express admiration for *La Parisienne,* said nothing and Henri Céard, who was to become almost hostile to the playwright, was equally taciturn.

A few impartial critics–Edouard Thierry and the poets Henri de Bornier and François Coppée–defended the play against its detractors and protested the cutting of the last two scenes. They rightly pointed out that to end the play with Teissier's innocuous words to Madame

Vigneron in Scene VIII ("And in three weeks your second daughter will be called Madame Teissier") and to suppress the final scene, where Teissier, after upbraiding one of the vultures, warns Marie that she is surrounded by scoundrels after the death of her father, was to greatly weaken the irony on which the ending depends.

Several discerning critics were struck by the similarity of Becque's *procédé* to that of Molière. Louis Ganderax, writing in the influential *Revue des Deux Mondes,* was one of the first to compare the characters of *Les Corbeaux* with those of the seventeenth-century dramatist and to note Becque's resemblance to Molière in power of observation and psychological penetration.[5] A few years later, after the revival of *Les Corbeaux* at the Odéon in 1897, Jules Lemaître expressed much the same opinion. A number of more recent critics have been in complete agreement. Ambroise Got is among those who have termed the play "a comedy of character in the grand classic style," and Eric Dawson in 1922 and Paul Blanchart in 1930 both insisted on Becque's resemblance to Molière.

Becque himself seemed uncertain how to classify *Les Corbeaux.* While writing the play he called it a "melodrama"; in 1880 he labeled it a "comédie-drame," in 1881 a "comédie," and in 1882 a "play in four acts." Finally in his *Théâtre complet* he returns to the term "comédie."

Even had Becque given the play a happy conclusion by resorting to the deus ex machina ending of *Tartuffe* or *L'Avare,* he would not have succeeded in converting it into a comedy. Where Molière achieved comic effect by insisting on the comic fault of his protagonist and by subjecting that fault to ridicule, Becque achieves a more tragic effect by insisting on the weakness and the moral suffering of his victims, while at the same time portraying in ironic fashion the comic faults of their oppressors. Without this double perspective *Les Corbeaux* might easily have been reduced to mere pathos. As it is, Becque avoids the pathos of the realistic drama of the eighteenth century as well as the moralism, the declamatory style, and the tendency to melodrama that stamps both the *drame bourgeois* and the *comédie larmoyante.*

To Paul Hervieu, a distinguished critic and playwright of Becque's own day, *Les Corbeaux* was neither a comedy nor a drama. In his opinion the play marked a return to tragedy, but to a tragedy that had been stripped of its purple pall and renewed by contact with modern life and thought:

Gloomy and overpowering, it returns instinctively to tragedy, but to a tragedy whose renovation has been suggested by modern conditions: no longer in the grand manner, but contemporary, rational, prosaic. . . . Needless to say, fatality . . . is no longer manifested, as among the Greeks, through dreams, visions, omens, oracles, or the Furies. But today one seeks to reveal the fatal manner in which the struggle for survival crushes the imprudent, the defenseless, the impassioned.[6]

There is much to be said in support of Hervieu's thesis. The tragedy of the Vigneron family is indeed a "struggle for survival which crushes the imprudent, the defenseless, and the impassioned." It is a tragedy which, as Hervieu maintained, is dictated by modern conditions, by a society whose values are the product of a Darwinian age. "You have undergone the law of the survival of the fittest, and that's all," Bourdon says to Madame Vigneron in explaining the loss of the family fortune. And that law, he could have added, had been as inexorable as the Greek nemesis. Curiously enough, Ambroise Got, while designating *Les Corbeaux* a "comedy of character in grand classic style," describes it in a way that confirms Bourdon's words and suggests the definition of modern tragedy ventured by Hervieu: "It is a picture of the bitter struggle for life, the day to day struggle for daily bread, the strong who devour the weak; it is the breakdown of law, of right, and of justice."[7]

If *Les Corbeaux* has been seen by some as a sort of modern tragedy, Marie may be viewed as the heroine of that tragedy–the Antigone of an age whose values are purely physical and material. Both Antigone and Marie act in accord with a sense of duty dictated by their conscience. But for Antigone, mere existence was only a trivial value as compared with those spiritual values which gave existence its only justification. Marie, on the other hand, sacrifices her happiness in order to allow her family to continue an existence which Antigone in similar circumstances would have scorned.

Both are prompted to self-sacrifice by nobility of heart and by devotion to their loved ones. Both leave the spectator with a certain feeling of optimistic belief in human nature. And both, despite the tragic outcome of their situation, are proof that goodness and virtue are not nonexistent and that, in the unequal contest with injustice and evil, they can never be completely destroyed.

CHAPTER 5

La Parisienne (Woman of Paris)

I Its Interpreters

IN December, 1882 a news item in *Le Réveil* disclosed the fact that the author of *Les Corbeaux* was completing a comedy entitled *La Parisienne.* It was not until three years later, however, that Becque, after long and arduous work, actually submitted the play to the Comédie-Française for acceptance. Despite the fact that Perrin, the director of the Comédie, had asked him for a new play, differing in tone and in genre from that of *Les Corbeaux*, and despite the enthusiastic support of the actor Coquelin, the play was rejected by a vote of six to three.[1] The disappointed author met with no more success at the Vaudeville, where a play by Labiche was chosen in preference to *La Parisienne.* Finally, in desperation, Becque offered his comedy to Adolphe Louveau, a former actor at the Odéon, who, under the pseudonym of Fernand Samuel, had taken over the Renaissance theater and was looking for a suitable production.

As usual, Becque insisted on coaching the terrified actors and drove them almost to distraction by his demands. To Mademoiselle Antonine who created the role of Clotilde and who asked about a passage that she did not understand, the irate author is said to have answered caustically: "Don't worry, that's the one you do best."[2] On the whole, however, the acting was better than Becque was willing to admit, and Antonine succeeded far better than Suzanne Reichemberg, who was to play the part in a revival of the play at the Comédie-Française in 1890.

The play opened on February 7, 1885 and proved an immediate success. The obvious approval of the public, however, did not deter certain critics from accusing Becque of pessimism and immorality. The fact that the Naturalists were almost lyrical in their praise and that Zola had hailed the play as a masterpiece only encouraged them in the belief that *La Parisienne* was a product of Naturalism at its worst. Sarcey, whom Becque considered his archenemy, admitted the popular success of the comedy but failed to give his approval. Though he later grew quite enthusiastic after having seen the play for a third and fourth time, Becque, far from being mollified, was even more adamant in his contempt for the well-known critic.

On June 7, 1888, *La Parisienne* was performed at the salon of Madame Aubernon with Réjane and Antoine playing the leading roles. In *Mes Souvenirs sur le Théâtre-Libre,* Antoine tells how Becque was enchanted by Réjane's verve and spirit and how, when there was any disagreement between them about the interpretation, Becque would settle the matter by putting his arm around her waist and waltzing her gaily around the room.[3]

Although the revival of *La Parisienne* at the Comédie-Française in 1890 was marred by the false interpretation and artificial diction of actors accustomed to the grand manner of classical drama, it met with complete success three years later at the Vaudeville, where Réjane again interpreted the role of Clotilde with brilliant understanding and insight. On April 19, 1899, about a month before Becque's death, it proved highly successful at the Théâtre-Antoine with Antoine himself acting the part of Lafont. Since that date, *La Parisienne* has been frequently seen both in France and abroad. In 1967, it was given a brilliant performance on television with Nicole Courcel as Clotilde, Jean Poiret as Lafont, and Pierre Mondy as Adolphe.

II *Its Sources*

It is often argued that *La Parisienne* represents Becque's cynical view of women and of love. The dramatist's grand-nephew, Jean Robaglia, admits that Becque had a poor opinion of women and recalls his answer to an interlocutor who had asked the dramatist if he believed all women were like Clotilde. "Objectively, of course, I have no idea," he is said to have replied, "but judging from what I have seen around me, everything proves it" (I, 42).

Despite Becque's sardonic response, there is no reason to believe that *La Parisienne* is indicative of his attitude toward all women. His deep attachment to his mother and sister, the solid virtues he attributes to Madame Chevalier in *Les Honnêtes Femmes,* his almost tender portrayal of Madame Vigneron and her daughters, and his letter to Octave Mirbeau in 1889 in which he maintains that the Vigneron daughters were more typical of the average French girl than the heroines of most of his contemporaries, all are sufficient proof to the contrary.

There is every reason then to believe that Becque was sincere in affirming that he wrote *La Parisienne* because critics, directors, and the theatergoing public preferred to see only "frivolity and broad humor" on the French stage: "If *Les Corbeaux* had been played when it should have been, that is to say when it was finished, I should never have written *La Navette.* And later, after the performance of *Les Corbeaux,* if Perrin had been a different man, I would have given *Le Monde d'argent [The World of Finance]* to the Théâtre-Français and I would never have written *La Parisienne"* (II, 338).

To critics who accused him of using a title that seemed to put all French women in a category with Clotilde, he answered in evident disgust: "To want me to call my play *Une Parisienne* is to want to have me make a grammatical mistake. Molière didn't write *Un Misanthrope* but *Le Misanthrope;* he didn't write *Quelques Femmes savantes [Some Learned Ladies]* but *Les Femmes savantes."*[4] As a matter of fact, Becque was not the first to use the title *La Parisienne.* In 1691 Dancourt had called one of his plays by the same title, and in 1907 Brieux was to use one very similar, *La Française.*

Objections to the title *La Parisienne* did not cease with the passing of the years. Between 1914 and 1918 the play was not presented in France under the pretext that it was derogatory to French women. Between 1935 and 1945 it was called *Clotilde,* and, when the play was given in London in 1934, a reviewer remarked that it did as much harm to the French as the *affaire Staviski.*[5]

Even though *La Parisienne* was not intended as an indictment of all French women, it obviously reflected the moral standards of a certain segment of society with which Becque was familiar. A passage from an article on divorce which he published in *Le Matin* on September 14, 1884 can almost be taken as a résumé of the play:

> The charming world of adultery is not about to come to an end. There is something frivolous and transient about a love affair that married women will not forego. They will not forego anything at all. Those who have status, a family, their social circle, a whole set-up to which they are accustomed and which marriage has created will not abandon it rashly. Ah, any other folly but that! Many women, moreover, who deceive their husbands with real enthusiasm, would hesitate to marry their lover. If the lover were jealous, for example, they wouldn't want to do so at any price. (V, 159)

It is just such a woman that Becque portrays in *La Parisienne,* and there is no more reason to believe that he considers Clotilde typical of all women than to believe that Molière considered Célimène or Agnès typical of all seventeenth-century women.

III *Technique*

La Parisienne is brilliantly constructed, yet so simple, so devoid of all but psychological action that it has been called more classic than any play of Molière.[6] In a sense, it is only a longer version of *La Navette.* Antonia, the courtesan of the earlier one-act play, has become Clotilde, the middle-class wife and mother of a three-act play. It is the story of a woman who drops her lover in the first act and takes him back in the last. In the meantime, she is abandoned by her new lover, and her husband, through the influence of his wife's friend, Madame Simpson, obtains the position to which he aspires.

The lack of action came as a surprise to Becque's contemporaries and was met with admiration on one hand and consternation on the other. Zola, who in his *Naturalism au Théâtre* had called for a return to simplicity of action, acclaimed the play a masterpiece. Henry Bauër, Octave Mirbeau, and Jules Lemaître were equally enthusiastic in their praise. A few critics complained that the play had no beginning, middle, or end; others that it lacked a climax and a denouement. Unlike *Les Corbeaux,* which was far more traditional in its technique, *La Parisienne* is really "a slice of life" in which, as Gérard Bauër points out, the absence of events and of a crisis arises from the determination of Clotilde to avoid any change and to maintain the status quo.[7]

Far from resulting in monotony, the lack of action seems only to call more attention to the duel of wits and to the sparkling dialogue. The first act is one of the most brilliant and amusing in modern drama. There are no explanations, no long *récits*, no *confidants* to brief the audience. On the contrary, Becque employs the very *procédé* that he had admired in Molière: "He [Molière] thrusts some characters on the stage and it is these characters who explain themselves to us. How? By being alive" (VII, 10).

The opening scene is a dazzling piece of virtuosity in which Becque tricks the spectators into believing that they are witnessing a quarrel between a jealous husband and his wife. Not until the last line do they discover that the jealous husband is actually the jealous lover. Clotilde rushes on stage, hides a letter under the blotter on a table, then goes to a writing desk and, taking a key from her pocket, pretends to be locking the desk. She is followed by Lafont, who, angry and distraught, commands her to open the desk and give him the letter. Clotilde refuses; Lafont grows more desperate. The quarrel becomes more animated as Lafont insists either on seeing the letter or on knowing where Clotilde has been. Finally in an outburst of passionate eloquence, he pleads: "Think of me, Clotilde, and think of yourself. Remember that a mistake is easily made and that it is never repaired. Don't give in to that taste for intrigue which is making so many victims today. Resist, Clotilde, resist! By remaining faithful to me, you remain worthy and respectable; the day you deceive me . . ." (Act I, sc. 1).

At that moment Clotilde cuts him short, goes quickly to the door, and returns with the warning: "Watch out. Here comes my husband." And the scene ends abruptly, as the audience, taken by surprise, explodes into laughter.

The demanding lover jealous of the husband was a reversal of the usual dramatic situation and adds a sharp note of irony which Becque exploits to the fullest throughout the play. Though nothing really happens in the course of the three acts, the interest of the spectator is never allowed to flag. The significance of the date January 15, the means by which Clotilde will obtain the position for her husband, the plight of the frustrated lover, and the question whether du Mesnil will discover or whether he already suspects his wife's infidelity, all stimulate the curiosity of the audience and are parts of a puzzle that are not completely solved until the end of the play.

But though *La Parisienne* lacks the feverish activity of the "well-made play," the byplay of the actors, so reminiscent of Molière, creates the illusion of action while adding to the comic effect: Lafont's indecision about accepting the keys for the desk, which Clotilde throws across the room and defies him to pick up at the risk of her displeasure; Clotilde's triumph as she waves the letter (which turns out to be from her conniving friend Pauline) and taunts Lafont from behind her husband's back; the shocked glances exchanged between husband and lover as Clotilde tells them of Mrs. Simpson's "liberal" views; Lafont's inability to carry out his intention to leave as he starts to go and then retraces his steps, much like Valère as he quarrels with Mariane in *Le Tartuffe.*

But it is the irony, which Becque uses with devastating results, that mainly accounts for the comic effects. Much of the irony derives from the incongruity between what the characters do and what they say. With all the moral eloquence of a *raisonneur* in a play of Dumas *fils,* Lafont urges Clotilde to resist all temptation and to remain faithful to him; Clotilde reminds her husband of her concern for his welfare ("I don't know any husband who is more pampered than you") and emphasizes her importance to his needs ("What would become of you if you ran into real trouble? If you lost me, for example! . . ." Especially amusing is Clotilde's sincere and frank insistence on her conservative or even reactionary tastes: "I like order, tranquility, and well established principles. I want churches to be open in case I feel like going into one. I also want the shops to be open and full of pretty things so that I may have the pleasure of seeing them even if I can't buy." At the same time, she is genuinely shocked by Lafont's liberal tendencies: "You are a free thinker! I imagine you would get along fine with a mistress who had no religion. How disgusting!" (Act I, sc. 3).

Lafont, on his part, feels a certain kinship with the man he is betraying: "When I feel despondent and when Clotilde upsets me, there is no one I would rather be with than her husband. I feel less lonely. Adolphe's position consoles me a little for my own; it's not as good as mine; it is certainly not as good" (Act II, sc. 4). And to Clotilde, who he thinks has deceived him, he remarks tearfully: "Ah, Clotilde! What have you done? You should have deceived me delicately, without telling me and without my seeing it" (Act II, sc. 9).

Often the characters seem quite unconscious of the incongruous effect of their remarks. At other times, the irony seems deliberate, motivated by a mischievous or even malicious intent, as when Clotilde assures Lafont that she no longer intends to dine with him surreptitiously while pretending to her husband that she is visiting a former school friend: "I decided that these escapades in restaurants had all kinds of drawbacks. They involve me in lies that are revolting and that I don't want to continue. Don't you think I'm right?" (Act II, sc. 5).

No finer example of deliberate irony can be found than at the end of the play when Lafont is taken back into the good graces of Clotilde, and the two explain Lafont's long absence to du Mesnil by inventing an unfortunate love affair. When du Mesnil insists on knowing whether or not Lafont had been betrayed by his mistress, the suspicious lover answers, with Clotilde in mind: "What do you expect me to answer? Is there any man who could swear that his mistress never deceived him? Mine said she hadn't. She could hardly say she had. We had a reconciliation; that's what we both wanted evidently" (Act III, sc. 7).

Clotilde, understanding perfectly, cannot resist teasing the wary Lafont: "It's too bad the lady isn't present to hear you; she would find out your opinion of her and of all women. You must have confidence, Monsieur Lafont, that's the only system that works with us." And the play ends with a remark by du Mesnil that leaves the audience wondering whether he is merely naïve or whether he too has an inkling of the real situation: "That's always been my system, my dear."

Whereas the irony in the case of Clotilde and Lafont is the result of their attempts either to deceive or to tease, in the case of du Mesnil it usually takes the form of pompous remarks that reveal his self-complacency. The author of a book *Considérations sur le budget,* he solemnly explains that one hundred and nineteen copies had been sold or, quickly correcting himself, really one hundred and eighteen, since one copy, which could not be found, had evidently been stolen. And when he reluctantly agrees to Clotilde's plan to use Madame Simpson's influence in obtaining the position he desires, he adds in his most pompous manner: "If Lolotte succeeds where a member of the Institute has failed, I shall be delighted personally, but I shall be sorry for France" (Act II, sc. 7).

Throughout the play the dialogue is so natural that the spectator has the impression of overhearing a real-life conversation. Especially remarkable is Becque's ability to shock or surprise the audience without resorting to strong or coarse language. Strangely enough, there is not a single prurient line to be found in the entire play.

IV *Characters*

Even more than *Les Corbeaux, La Parisienne* is proof of Becque's belief that the best plays are those that center on character portrayal. In Clotilde, he has created a universal type who is as timeless as Célimène or Agnès. In contrast with the Vigneron daughters, who, unlike the average French girl of today, were unable to support themselves or to cope with financial problems, Clotilde is as true to life and as typical of a certain segment of contemporary society as she was in 1885.

One of the reasons for the fascination of the play is the fact that Becque makes no attempt to supply us with a key to her character. Nothing said by others or even by herself—except quite indirectly—explains her psychology or her motivation. Perhaps because Becque remains so completely detached and impersonal, Clotilde's enigmatic character has been subjected to various interpretations, which, to a great extent, depend upon the actress who plays the role. Of all those who have attempted the part, no one has succeeded more brilliantly than Réjane, who, playing with Antoine, as Lafont, at the Vaudeville in 1893, made the play an uncontested success and erased the false impression that had resulted from its presentation in the grand style of the Comédie-Française three years earlier. Becque himself was delighted with her performance, though he was not always in complete accord with her interpretation. In a letter to André Bernheim, written in November, 1890, the charming actress reveals the key to her interpretation: "I don't think it's necessary to probe too deeply into Clotilde: we must get it clearly into our minds that we are playing the role of a 'bourgeoise' with the instincts of a prostitute and of a prostitute who has no consciousness of her actions."[8]

It is interesting to note that Becque seems to have slightly changed his conception of the play when it was presented in 1899, shortly before his death. To Madame Devoyod, who was preparing to play Clotilde, with Antoine as Lafont, he is said to have remarked: "*La Parisienne* is a *drame,* a *drame* which is played in the heart and the mind. If you play it, don't make it comic: you will betray me. Forget and make others forget that I may have put some wit into the text."[9] Just why Becque spoke as he did is difficult to explain, for his change of viewpoint is hard to reconcile with the play as it is written.

Critics and spectators have differed as much as performers in their understanding of Clotilde and have judged her to be everything from a monster of perversity to a *petite bourgeoise,* willing to take a lover in order to advance the best interests of her husband. As portrayed by Becque, however, she is neither one nor the other. Her affairs with both Lafont and Simpson are certainly not motivated by mercenary reasons, for she gives no evidence of avarice or even of a desire to obtain greater luxuries than she already has. On the contrary, she seems fond of her home and her husband and perfectly content with what her present life has to offer her.

Nor does she show any sensuality either in words or in conduct. If anything, she gives the impression of being more cerebral than passionate. It is, in fact, this lack of overpowering passion on the one hand and of greed or avarice on the other that sets her apart from the adulteress of previous dramas and makes her so difficult to understand. Clotilde has sometimes been compared to Jacqueline in *Le Chandelier,* and the comparison is entirely valid in certain respects. But though Clotilde possesses the diabolical cleverness of Musset's heroine, she completely lacks the wistful appeal shown by the latter in her relationship to Fortunio. And quite unlike Jacqueline, she never allows her head to be ruled by her heart.

Although most critics find Clotilde incapable of genuine emotion or sincerity, Descotes believes that, in her parting scene with Simpson, she is moved by "profound emotion" and shows signs of "true sadness."[10] Arnaoutovitch, likewise, maintains that Clotilde is greatly saddened in breaking with her newly acquired lover and that the scene contains "a note of deep sorrow."[11] Réjane's interpretation would tend to support their idea, for it is said that at this point in the play she would break down and burst into uncontrollable sobs. There seems to be no justification for this interpretation in the text, however, and it may well explain Becque's reservations about the performance.

It is true that Clotilde sheds a few tears as Simpson is preparing to leave, for he suddenly turns to her and asks if she is weeping. Clotilde admits that she is weeping "very sincerely" and, on being asked why, replies with words that might have been spoken by a heroine straight out of Musset: "Who knows? There is a little of everything in a woman's tears" (Act III, sc. 1). The lines that follow show a certain nostalgia–melancholy even–but certainly not deep emotion. Even more significant is her long monologue spoken immediately after Simpson's departure:

What a stupid affair! None of the young men today are worth bothering about. They are hard, full of pretentions, believe in nothing; they are show-offs, that's all. I thought that Monsieur Simpson, brought up by his mother, would become seriously attached to a woman. I have no reason to complain about him, however. He has always been very mannerly and very obliging .... He's a bit dull on the subject of his guns. ... (Act III, sc. 4)

The words leave little doubt that it is not so much sorrow or grief that Clotilde feels as irritation and disappointment.

Moreover, her immediate readiness to dismiss Simpson from her mind and to take back Lafont are hardly symptomatic of any real heartbreak. She continues:

It served me right. I had what I needed, an excellent friend, a second husband, so to speak. I mistreated him in all sorts of ways, and he got tired of it, which is natural. Who knows? He may think me angrier than I am; men don't understand us very well. We have a weakness, it's true, for the one we like, but we always come back to the one who loves us. (Act III, sc. 4)

Although it is clear that neither mercenary motives nor any deep sensuality motivate the actions of Clotilde, the actual reasons for her conduct are less apparent. Only twice in the play does she give any hint about her attitude. In her conversation with Lafont in Act II, she alludes to her need for something more than the ordinary fare of everyday domestic life: "Like all women, I dreamed of an ideal existence in which I could fulfill my duties without sacrificing my heart; a sort of heaven and earth." And in her parting conversation with Simpson, it becomes even more evident that her extramarital affairs are a means of escaping the monotony of life: "Life [without a love affair] wouldn't perhaps be very amusing or very exciting, but we would avoid many worries, many disillusions, many regrets" (Act III, sc. 2).

For Clotilde, a love affair is obviously a sort of game which is wrong only if she gets caught or if she neglects her duties to her husband or family. She is displeased by what she believes to be Lafont's indifference to du Mesnil and angrily accuses him of not liking her husband. And when Simpson, before his departure, urges her to come and visit him in Croquignole, she refuses with almost shocked surprise. To leave her husband to fare for himself would not be following the rules of the game and could also be taking unnecessary risks. When told by Simpson that her friend Pauline had no such scruples, she answers with the only logic that she knows: "It's different with Pauline. First of all, she has a fortune which permits her to do what she wants. Then, her husband has wronged her badly; she takes advantage of it and she is quite right" (Act III, sc. 2).

Clotilde has no reason for taking similar advantage of her husband. In fact, she is fond of him in her own way and even puts his interests before her own pleasure. Although she calls him a "Bovary," it is with a sort of fond tolerance, and, unlike Emma Bovary, she makes every effort to preserve his dignity and happiness. When she wishes to be alone, she orders her maid, Adèle, to admit no visitor unless it be someone for her husband. And when du Mesnil unexpectedly returns home, dejected at the prospect of not obtaining the position for which he is hoping, Clotilde gives up her rendezvous and insists on listening to his troubles. It is true that she is somewhat apprehensive, fearing that her husband may have discovered her infidelity, but, once her fears prove groundless, she is anxious to be of assistance, especially since she intends to call upon the aid of Simpson and his influential mother whose dubious company du Mesnil had hitherto shunned.

It has been suggested by certain critics, including Jules Lemaître, that Clotilde's liaison with Simpson was prompted by her desire to assure a lucrative position for her husband and thus to advance his interests.[12] This idea, however, is actually contradicted by the text, for it is clear that her affair with Simpson had begun before the question of du Mesnil's position arose. Clotilde herself reminds Simpson that she had become his mistress before any favor had been done her husband.

Moreover, once Clotilde learns of her husband's predicament, she is quite happy to be of service to him. In fact, the occasion is only further proof in her eyes of the wisdom of her conduct and of her belief that a woman's place is not exclusively in the home: "Talk about modesty and reserve in a woman! What nonsense! What would my husband have done, if he hadn't had me?" (Act II, sc. 8).

Throughout the play it is obvious that Clotilde feels no sense of guilt, contrary to the belief of Arnaoutovitch that she is "a prey to an inner struggle between Good and Evil."[13] It is true that in her conversations with Lafont and Simpson she uses such words as "fault" and "guilty" in alluding to her situation, but, for her, the words are only euphemisms, and it is clear that her conscience is not involved in the slightest degree.

The clue to Clotilde's psychology and to her moral evaluation of her liaisons becomes apparent in the reproach she addresses to the too insistent Lafont: "You must realize that I am not free, that I have a house to take care of and relations to maintain; bagatelles only come afterwards" (Act I, sc. 3). For Clotilde, extramarital love is only a "bagatelle" with no more, no less significance. As long as she preserves appearances and fulfills her wifely duties, she has no sense of guilt, no feeling of wrongdoing. In this respect, Réjane seemed quite correct in viewing Clotilde as an ordinary middle-class housewife with the instincts of a prostitute who has no consciousness of her actions. Jules Lemaître expressed much the same idea when he compared Clotilde to "millions of creatures among us who remain untouched by any morality or religion, although they ingenuously follow certain social rites."[14]

When Lafont apologizes for his suspicions and his jealousy by explaining that "it is love that makes me that way," Clotilde is even capable of denigrating love: "Love can be a nuisance!" (Act II, sc. 5). Yet she is not entirely lacking in sympathy, annoying as she finds his persistence. "I'm always afraid of seeing him weep," she remarks to herself, as he leaves. "He looks pretty sad, with his head hanging down. Poor fellow! I'll pay him a little visit tomorrow" (Act II, sc. 6).

There is even evidence that Clotilde is quite aware of the inconsistency of men's logic in holding to the double standard and that she is knowingly playing their game. When Lafont criticizes Pauline for betraying her husband, Clotilde reminds him that he is reproaching her friend for being to her lover what she, Clotilde, is to him. Moreover, she has few illusions and even suspects Simpson of having tried to pay court to Pauline.

Curiously enough, Clotilde seems much amused by her own game, and both her actions and words remind us of her remark to Simpson that, without a liaison, life wouldn't be as "amusing or exciting." In carrying on her extramarital affairs, she seems to take a special pleasure in telling unnecessary lies. Moreover, like Jacqueline in *Le Chandelier,* she does so with the greatest ease and delight. When she is with du Mesnil and Lafont, she pokes fun at Lafont and remarks *sotto voce* to her husband: "He gets on my nerves, but he amuses me. His nose makes me want to laugh. I wouldn't want a man with a nose like that to kiss me" (Act I, sc. 2). Or again she whispers to du Mesnil when Simpson is out of earshot: "He [Simpson] is not the sort of person who would make me forget my duties" (Act III, sc. 3).

She seems to take a special pleasure in tormenting the hapless Lafont in every possible way. To excite his jealousy, she pretends to hide an innocuous letter which she later has her husband read aloud, or she makes tantalizing references to January 15, which the reader will discover marked the beginning of her liaison with Simpson. At another time she promises to follow Lafont to his apartment, then, after his departure, orders Adèle to bring her robe and slippers and refuse admittance to any visitor.

Clotilde is especially amusing when she tells half-truths which go unrecognized by those involved. To du Mesnil she explains Lafont's long absence and sudden return by telling him that their old friend had been made too unhappy by jealousy of his mistress to appear at their home. And when Lafont, queried by du Mesnil, admits that he doesn't know whether or not he had been betrayed, Clotilde smugly reminds him that he ought to be more trusting.

One of the most amusing scenes is that in which Clotilde advises her husband to use Madame Simpson's influence in obtaining the position that he desires. When du Mesnil tells her how a friend had been promoted ahead of him, Clotilde suggests disapprovingly the dubious means by which the position must have been obtained—the very means which she herself intends to employ:

Clotilde—Is he married?
du Mesnil—What does that have to do with it?
Clotilde—Tell me anyway.
du Mesnil—Yes, he's married.
Clotilde—His wife is young?
du Mesnil—About your age.
Clotilde—Pretty?
du Mesnil—Attractive.

Clotilde–Easy-going?
du Mesnil–That's what they say.
Clotilde–The hussy!
du Mesnil–I see.
Clotilde–It's about time. (Act II, sc. 7)

In comparison with Clotilde, Lafont and du Mesnil are far less complex and interesting. Du Mesnil, in particular, borders on the farcical, blind as he is to all that is going on under his nose. Yet, though he has sometimes been played as the complete idiot, he is much less a caricature than the bumbling husband of Jacqueline in *Le Chandelier.* His pomposity, the seriousness with which he views himself as an author, and his self-complacency are not uncommon foibles. His very egoism makes it difficult for him to believe that someone else could be preferred to him–all the more so since Clotilde shows herself so clever in her deceit.

Moreover, by the end of the play the spectator is not entirely sure if du Mesnil is as blind as he first appears. As in the case of Clotilde, much depends upon the interpretation of the actor. The last line of the play, spoken by du Mesnil to Clotilde, has a somewhat ambiguous character, as has been noted, and leaves the audience curious as to its real meaning. When Clotilde reminds Lafont that the best system with women is to have confidence in them, her husband adds somewhat enigmatically: "That's always been mine, my dear." Intentional or fatuous–the remark could be either, and all depends upon the manner in which the words are spoken. The suspicion arises that du Mesnil may be too satisfied with his lot to wish to change and that he has deliberately closed his eyes to the truth, knowing that in any event he is happier than his friend and rival, Lafont. It is even more probable that he is perhaps too obtuse and too complacent to suspect that he is the dupe of his wife and closest friend.

In his portrait of Lafont, Becque has shown striking originality and has created a character who, like Clotilde, has furnished a new source of comedy to later writers. In portraying a lover who is as much a cuckold as the husband and in making the husband and lover close friends, who share a mutual interest in keeping Clotilde away from the unhealthy influence of a corrupt society, Becque has discovered a new and rich vein of humor. Lafont's plea to Clotilde to resist temptation and remain faithful to him, his shocked surprise, and the meaningful glances that he exchanges with du Mesnil, as the latter reads the letter from Pauline describing Madame Simpson's tolerant and "broad-minded" views, his tacit feeling of camaraderie with du Mesnil in being duped by Clotilde, all are broadly comic as well as deeply ironic.

Like Clotilde, he seems completely unaware of any moral wrong in his own actions, though he does not hesitate to judge his mistress and to remind her of her wrongs toward her husband. Far from believing that he has betrayed his friend, he has a warm liking for him and finds in his company his only consolation when Clotilde makes him the most unhappy.

Like Alfred and Arthur in *La Navette,* he is pathetically concerned with maintaining his dignity and respectability, and, like them, he is proof of what Chevillard had remarked to his friend Delaunay in *L'Enfant prodigue:* "We are all a little stupid when it comes to women" (Act III, sc. 2). It is his very insistence on respectability as well as his constant jealousy that makes Clotilde find him something of a bore and leads her to remark: "I don't have any peace any more except when my husband is here" (Act II, sc. 10). For Clotilde, the affair has taken on all the seriousness of marriage–the very thing that she has been trying to escape–and Lafont has come to be in her eyes "a second husband, so to speak."

V *Its Originality*

With *La Parisienne,* Becque has moved even further from the social theater of Dumas *fils* and Augier and has given a new conception of the courtesan which differs radically from that of his predecessors. It is the woman herself–her psychology and moral temperament–that inspires his drama, rather than the social preoccupations to which the problem of the courtesan gives rise.

Moreover, the author of *La Parisienne* has carried objectivity to its furthest point, for he reveals the moral turpitude of his characters only in what they do and say, while leaving to the spectator the task of formulating any moral judgment. The morality lies not in what the protagonists think of themselves or in what they say of each other but in what the spectator discovers for himself. The author neither condemns nor condones. Instead, he practices what he so often preached: "The theater is not a means of teaching a moral lesson. The theater is a painting, a representation" (VII, 40).

In its dispassionate objectivity, its emphasis on psychology, its simplicity of action, and its use of the "slice-of-life" technique, *La Parisienne* came to represent a model for the new drama and opened the way for the *comédie rosse* of the Théâtre-Libre. With *Les Corbeaux,* it explains why Antoine and his disciples viewed Becque as their master, even though they themselves never succeeded in attaining the same impeccable artistry.

CHAPTER 6

Late Plays

I Veuve! (Widowed!)

LA *Parisienne* was the last play which Becque was to offer to the theater. Though he continued to write articles and reviews for various newspapers, he seemed incapable of further serious literary production. His deteriorating health, his literary quarrels, his lectures and articles, and his newly begun social life in which he took almost childlike pleasure, all help to explain the decline of his dramatic power. Whatever the cause, after 1885 Becque completed only five short one-act plays–too slight to be of any real importance–and worked sporadically on a long serious drama, *Les Polichinelles (The Puppets),* which he never succeeded in finishing.

Veuve!, a sort of epilogue in ten pages to *La Parisienne,* was published in *La Vie Parisienne* on March 20, 1897. It depends for its interest on the ironic portrayal of its characters and, at the same time, tantalizes the reader by suggesting certain enigmas which are left unsolved.

Du Mesnil is dead and Clotilde receives a visit from Lafont, her lover and husband's close friend. As moved by the death of du Mesnil as by the thought that Clotilde had been left alone for two days without the presence of one who loved her, Lafont questions his mistress about the tragic event. "Dear Adolphe, didn't he ever suspect anything?" he asks, and Clotilde answers simply, "Who knows?"

During his brief visit, the ever-jealous Lafont is visibly disturbed by a series of suspicious events. Clotilde tells him she intends to spend a month with her mother-in-law, leaving the children in Paris to pursue their studies. An amusing letter arrives from Pauline which Clotilde refuses to show her lover who is shocked by such levity at so serious a moment. After telling Lafont that her husband had suggested that she find security by marrying his long-time friend, she quickly adds that she has no intention of remarriage. A moment later, the maid announces the arrival of a funeral wreath from Monsieur Simpson, and Clotilde hastens to assure the suspicious Lafont that the sender must have been *Madame* Simpson.

As Lafont takes his leave, Clotilde ponders a few seconds and then says quietly to herself: "If I had to choose . . . between my husband and him . . . he is perhaps the one that I would have preferred to lose." The curtain falls as Clotilde scornfully tosses aside a sentimental letter of sympathy sent by a woman who, after twenty-seven years, still mourns the loss of her husband. As a dramatic composition the sketch has little or no importance; as a pendant to *La Parisienne,* it adds to its irony and further emphasizes the amoral conduct of its protagonists.

II Madeleine

Madeleine is no more than a scene, about twelve pages in length, drawn from Les *Polichinelles* and published with slight modifications in *La Vie Parisienne* in 1896. Several years later, in 1899, it was played in the salon of Madame Lucien Muhlfeld by the well-known actresses Cécile Sorel and Suzanne Devoyod.

Madeleine, a former courtesan, who in *Les Polichinelles* is known as Madame Antoine, has secretly taken refuge with her young daughter in Auteuil where she cuts all ties with her sordid past and attempts to bring up her daughter to lead an honorable and respectable life. Discovered by Elise, a former friend, Madeleine tells of her deep concern for her daughter whom she had entrusted to the sisters of Sacré Coeur, after confessing to them her own past mistakes. The play is nothing more than a conversation between two women in which Becque contrasts the repentant and self-sacrificing Madeleine with the pleasure-loving Elise. Though it adds nothing to his reputation as a dramatist, it offers further evidence that the author was not as much a misogynist as he is usually pictured.

III Le Départ (The Departure)

Le Départ, published in *La Revue de Paris* on May 1, 1897, may well have been the first act of a longer play which Becque intended as a sort of modern *La Dame aux camélias.*

The scene takes place in a large dressmaking establishment where most of the young girls working as seamstresses dream of making a happy marriage but end up by taking a lover in order to escape their dreary existence. Blanche, an attractive young girl who has determined to remain honorable, refuses to accept the offer of a wealthy aristocrat who is willing to give her all the luxuries of life. The son of her employer has also fallen in love with Blanche and, when she refuses his advances, asks his father for permission to marry her. The father in high dudgeon sends his son off to England but, intrigued by the beauty of the young girl, offers to make her his mistress: "If you find me too boring or too decrepit, things won't go any farther." Blanche angrily rejects his offer and is promptly dismissed by her outraged employer.

To add to the irony, Auguste, the slow-witted and industrious errand boy, asks Blanche to marry him, hoping that they can set up an establishment of their own. Completely disillusioned by her experiences, Blanche leaves a note for her friend Marie telling her that she has decided to accept the Baron's offer and that she is leaving that night to become his mistress.

Le Départ has little to recommend it from the dramatic standpoint. Neither original nor adroit, its moral lesson is that of similar plays by Augier, Dumas *fils,* or Brieux: the impossibility of remaining virtuous when a young girl is obliged to earn her living and to eke out an existence on her pitifully small earnings. The situation is much the same as that of Marie and Teissier, but, set in its new and slight framework, it has neither the pathos nor the power of *Les Corbeaux.*

IV Une Exécution

Une Exécution, published in *La Vie Parisienne* on July 24, 1897, is a short sketch which faintly recalls Becque's first play, *L'Enfant prodigue.* Justin, the mayor's son, threatens to disgrace his parents by his unseemly conduct, his debts, his dishonesty, and his amorous adventures. In order to avoid further embarrassment, the father sends Justin to Paris. Presenting his son with a first-class ticket and a hundred francs with which to install himself in the city, the father lectures his son in a pontifical manner, somewhat reminiscent of Bernardin's farewell speech to Théodore. As the train pulls out of the station, the mayor heaves a sigh of relief and remarks: "Ouf! Well, that's settled! I was afraid of having a bad time of it!"

The play is a mere trifle—too slight to be taken seriously. The role of Justin, who appears just before the train is to leave, is limited to pantomime and that of the father depends for its comic effect on its heavy-handed humor and its cynical preachments.

V Le Domino à Quatre (Dominoes for Four)

Le Domino à Quatre, about eighteen pages in length, was published in *La Vie Parisienne,* March 20, 1897, and presented at the Odéon as late as June 1, 1908. Like Becque's other one-act plays, it is too slight to be of any real importance, though from the standpoint of technique it is surprisingly modern and original.

In the Café Alliance four friends meet every afternoon to play a game of dominoes. As the curtain opens, three of the four are seen: the husky Brocheton reading his newspaper, his hat on his head, and his glass of absinthe empty; Albanès, bald and lanky, with a glass of milk before him; and Savary, graying and plump, with his customary glass of beer. The three are awaiting the usually tardy Blanchart, whose precarious state of health, they all agree, augurs ill for the future. Brocheton insists Blanchart has abused his health with too many women, while Albanès keeps repeating mechanically, "He drugs himself too much." Blanchart arrives pale and disheveled–he had fallen down the steps–and, after ordering a sweet drink, joins the three in their game.

Scene II takes place a month later in the same café. Brocheton, the strongest of the four, is dead as a result of a heart attack, and Albarès and Savary, who are waiting for the sickly Blanchart, agree that the latter had never looked worse than at the funeral. Blanchart arrives, pale and out of breath. Though Savary is coming down with the grippe, he laughs at Blanchart's suggestion that he doctor himself and insists that dominoes is the best cure. They begin to play.

The third scene takes place a week later in the same café. Blanchart, alone, is waiting for Albanès. Savary is dead and had been buried that very morning. Albanès arrives and confides to his partner that Savary's health had been undermined by his wife's unfaithfulness. They begin to play.

Scene IV takes place three months later on a spring day in front of the Café Alliance. Blanchart, elegant and debonair, obviously in excellent health, stands before a kiosk, laughing heartily as he looks at the caricatures. A friend, who has returned from a long trip, happens along, and Blanchart jokingly tells him of his previous illnesses. The friend invites him to have a drink in the café, but Blanchart refuses, after telling him of the death of his three healthier companions. Albanès, the last of the three, he adds, had just been buried that very week. To his friend's suggestion that they go elsewhere, he replies gaily: "Not today . . . I am waiting for a lady!" The weakling has not only outlived his healthy friends; he is even indulging in the forbidden pleasures of the strong.

Of all Becque's one-act plays *Le Domino à quatre* is the most clever and original. Its novel subject, its skillful structure, its deliberately mechanical design and characters, its rapid-fire dialogue with its double meanings, all give it a refreshing quality and a sort of offbeat humor. It is only unfortunate that Becque was unable to match his novel technique with material of greater substance.

VI Les Polichinelles (The Puppets)

Two years after finishing *La Parisienne,* Becque set to work on a new drama which he hoped would surpass or at least equal his earlier masterpieces and become the crowning point of his career. Word quickly spread through the world of the theater that the author of *Les Corbeaux* and *La Parisienne* was writing a new play, and the public waited, with impatience and lively curiosity, for news of its progress.

For once Becque had no need to seek a producer; in 1890 Albert Carré of the Vaudeville asked permission to stage the play which, according to all accounts, was nearing completion. But Becque, to whom fame had come too late, was too worn out by years of struggle, too beset by ill health to realize his dream. Though he worked on it in a desultory fashion for a number of years, he seems to have abandoned his efforts by about 1893 and to have expended his fading energy on his lectures, his articles, and his role as a literary lion in the aristocratic salons where he was much in demand. The encouragement of his friends, their attempts to give him tranquility and temporary freedom from financial worries proved to be of no avail. Becque seemed unable to regain the zest and the creative power which he had shown so plainly in earlier years.

It seems obvious that Becque, who prided himself on his ability to develop new techniques, intended to use a format quite different from that of *La Parisienne* or *Les Corbeaux.* Whereas *La Parisienne* centered around three principal characters, *Les Polichinelles* was to have included about thirty. Whereas Clotilde and Lafont preserve the language and manners of the most respectable bourgeois society, the characters of *Les Polichinelles* reflect the vulgarity of the *comédie-rosse* both in their actions and in their speech.

Unfortunately, Becque never succeeded in finding the formula that was appropriate to his subject, for *Les Polichinelles* was never completed, and the fourth and fifth acts remain in fragmentary form. Though he invented a whole corrupt universe with which to people his drama, he was unable to find a suitable ending or even to successfully tie together what he had already written. He contented himself with publishing a few extracts and with reworking scene 15 of the third act, which he published on June 27, 1896 under the title of *Madeleine.*

Obviously, *Les Polichinelles* was to have been a satire on the world of finance and on the unscrupulous people who make up that world. Becque attempts not only to portray their base maneuvers in the financial world but also to reveal the dissipated lives that they led with their mistresses and acquaintances of the demimonde. What remains today shows none of its author's skill as a dramatist. On the contrary, its grim and humorless satire seems closer to the *comédie-rosse* of his contemporaries than anything else he has written.

Chief protagonist of *Les Polichinelles* is Tavernier, the unprincipled head of a foundering bank who has gone to Italy to obtain the financial backing needed to found another institution, the Bank of Naples, and thus to save himself from bankruptcy. In the opening scenes Tavernier's secretary is talking to Lombard, a police superintendent who threatens to bring action against the bank if it does not cease its dishonest practices. In Tavernier's office, friends and cohorts gather, anxiously awaiting the return of the banker. While they speculate as to the success of his mission, Marie, who is Tavernier's mistress, Toto, her lover of the moment, and Elise, her mother, join the group. Suddenly a loud voice is heard outside, and, in a scene reminiscent of the initial entrance of Tartuffe in Molière's famous play by that name, Tavernier arrives, calling out to his coachman: "I'll teach you to know who you're dealing with. I'm Tavernier the banker." Marie needs no further information. "He has succeeded," she announces to her companions.

Act II shows the police superintendent renewing his complaints just as Tavernier is about to take charge of a meeting of the administrative council of the Bank of Naples. A few moments later the meeting is interrupted by the arrival of Marie, who brings with her a young Hungarian girl and her lover. Marie introduces the girl as Bettina, and the meeting is broken up when the latter is persuaded to climb on a table and display her talents as a singer.

In Act III Marie, who has obtained the house for which she had been hounding Tavernier, is giving a housewarming party. The gaiety of the guests is dampened by news of the arrest of the banker Cerfbier, a friend and associate of Tavernier.

The last two acts show things going from bad to worse. Cerfbier has succeeded in escaping the clutches of the law, but Tavernier is in turn being threatened. Cerfbier refuses to come to the aid of Tavernier by merging his bank with that of his associate, and Tavernier is left alone to face one client after another who comes to demand reimbursement.

How Becque planned to complete the play has been a question of some debate. In 1910 Henri de Noussane supplied an ending in which Tavernier, by a daring business stroke, extricates himself from his precarious situation and is transformed into an honest man. A more unsuitable ending could hardly have been contrived, for from the very first scenes, it is clear that Becque's intention is to satirize a world made up of swindlers and "suckers" *(gogos),* a world in which evil and chicanery are triumphant.

As it stands, *Les Polichinelles* is monotonous, boring, and completely lacking in dramatic intensity, mainly because it lacks a clearly defined intrigue capable of tying together the many disparate elements and characters. Robaglia has suggested that Becque may have deliberately chosen to repudiate intrigue, since he was strongly opposed to the artificial theater of the day (IV, 85). However, there is little or no evidence in the play itself that Becque was attempting a "slice of life." On the contrary, everything seems to indicate an effort, however unsuccessful, to tie together the various events of the play with some semblance of a plot. Becque's mistake seems rather to stem from his conception and from his failure to carry out the precept which he stressed in a lecture on the theater in 1895; "Seriousness in the drama is not in the ideas. It is in the digestion of the ideas by the characters, in the dramatic or comic power which the characters give to the ideas" (VII, 76). Unfortunately, he is more interested in showing the complex and devious means by which the swindlers dupe their victims than in translating into human drama the causes or results of their financial machinations. The reader is lost in a maze of business details that have no more interest for him than the report of the stock market in the daily newspaper.

Moreover, Becque seems to have forgotten that, in the theater, satire cannot stand alone, that it must be reinforced by either comic or tragic elements, if it wishes to appeal to the audience. The powerful satire of *Les Corbeaux* is sharpened by our pity for the tragic plight of the victims. *La Parisienne* delights its audiences by combining satire with dry and irreverent humor. The irony in *Les Polichinelles,* on the contrary, is completely divorced from either comic or tragic elements and is not powerful enough to carry the weight of the play. In many respects, it is hardly more dramatic than the harsh and vitriolic observations of his *Querelles littéraires.*

Further weaknesses on Becque's part are his failure to reveal character through action and his excessive dependence on *récits* or anecdotes in which one character recounts the actions or life history of another. The play literally stands still while Elise relates the life story of Mont-les-Aigles, while Mont-les-Aigles, in turn, analyzes the character of Marie, and while Madame Antoine tells the story of her life to Elise.

As for style, Becque has abandoned the restraint of his earlier dramas and has adopted the coarse and vulgar language of the Naturalistic school. In addition, the play is filled with barbed witticisms directed at all of Becque's pet peeves–theater directors, journalists, financiers, corrupt government officials–which remind one of the maxims with which he delighted the salons in his last years. Marie's remark to Tavernier that to succeed as an actress "you have to wallow in the mire with everyone" is undoubtedly an overt reference to Sarcey to whose amorous affairs with actresses Becque often referred. Most typical of the author's corrosive wit is Tavernier's answer to Marie, who is curious to know whom Lombard has come to arrest: "How should I know? We are all in business." It is only in lines such as these that Becque shows some of the verve which had enlivened *La Parisienne.*

Becque has been no more successful in handling his characters than in developing the plot. With one or two exceptions, they differ little from each other except in the degree of their depravity. Nor could it have been otherwise, considering the large number that are introduced within so short a space of time. It is obvious that Becque has made an attempt to individualize his characters, and, in the case of the women, he has succeeded to a certain extent. Madame Antoine, who sacrifices her own interests in order to safeguard her daughter's future, Elise, who looks with pride on her profession and laments the changes in the present-day courtesan, differ from each other as much as they differ from Marie.

Marie, on the other hand, seems almost a monster of perversity. Domineering, grasping, callous, and demanding, her hold on Tavernier seems quite improbable. The scene in which she and her friends interrupt the business meeting and in which she orders Tavernier, in the presence of his associates, to give her five thousand francs and to show his subjection to her power by kissing her (she uses the verb *baiser* as opposed to *embrasser),* strains all credibility and verges, though quite unintentionally, on the comic.

The sure dramatic instinct which marked *La Parisienne* and *Les Corbeaux* seems almost completely absent in *Les Polichinelles,* and it is just as well that Becque never completed the play. Though he was aware of its deficiencies and worked hard to rectify them, he evidently failed to realize that it was his approach to the subject which was at fault and that only by changing that approach could he reach the dramatic heights he had attained in his two great masterpieces.

CHAPTER 7

Becque as a Critic

I *His Conception of Criticism and the Critics*

"THE great error of criticism and its insufferable pretentiousness is to believe that it is useful, efficacious, and salutary. It serves no purpose at all. Undoubtedly, it influences the immediate public, those who believe what is in print and who wait for newspaper articles to choose their play or their reading-matter. But the effect is only temporary; after a week it no longer exists. True judgment—that which is significant and lasting—is made in the salons and cafés" (VI, 71). Despite his belief that the theatergoing public was little influenced by critical reviews—a belief that his attacks on the popular drama critic Sarcey seem to belie—Becque himself served as a drama critic for various journals and newspapers between 1876 and 1893.

It is worthy of note that, of the seven volumes of his complete works, two and a half are devoted to his polemical writing and to his literary criticism. Of even greater importance is the little-known fact that Becque's esthetic ideas set him apart from critics of his own generation, such as Taine and Brunetière, and ally him in many respects with Baudelaire and Flaubert. His journalistic, down-to-earth mode of expression is closer to that of Flaubert in his correspondence than to that of Baudelaire who, unlike the author of *Les Corbeaux*, transformed criticism into a work of art through the magic of his style and his poetic sensibility.

Becque's own criticism is concerned almost entirely with the drama, though there are brief references to the novel and to poetry. Some of his articles are unfortunately colored by personal prejudice and animosity, especially those in which he treats the drama of Dumas *fils* or the criticism of Francisque Sarcey. His dislike for Sarcey in particular became a real obsession and revealed itself in attacks that were often savage, virulent, and crude. Becque even went so far as to attack the critic's personal life—in particular his affair with his young protégée Nancy Martel–and to accuse him of trying to destroy actresses who refused his advances.

Less offensive and far more amusing is Becque's brilliant pastiche of Sarcey's criticism in a mock review of Pradon's *Phèdre (Phaedra)* and Molière's *Le Tartuffe.* So clever was Becque in adopting the mannerisms and ideas of his contemporary and in imitating his style that an unknowing reader could easily believe he was reading one of Sarcey's own essays. By showing how the popular drama critic would have found *Tartuffe* dull, poorly constructed, and financially unprofitable, had it been written and presented in the nineteenth century, Becque effectively demonstrates the commercialism of the contemporary theater which Sarcey had done so much to encourage.

Becque's drama criticism is sometimes slight and uneven; at other times, lively and penetrating. Though he could be ferocious in attacking popular writers who were too well established to be seriously hurt, he was remarkably kind and encouraging to the young and inexperienced. In fact, his hostility to Sarcey and to Claretie, the director of the Comédie-Française, resulted in part from their tendency to accept only the old and the tried and to ignore what was new and original: "If the theater is in peril and in danger of disappearing, the fault lies with criticism as it is carried on today. . . . It [criticism] has been unscrupulous in dealing with newcomers. It has mocked all their efforts; it has disapproved all their attempts; Sarcey, even more brutal than the others, has gone so far as to aim at their pocketbook" (VI, 77, 79).

Baudelaire had maintained that the poet or creative artist is naturally and inevitably a critic. Becque goes even further and insists that the creative artist is the best of all critics. Critics, he affirms, have always been divided into two camps: university professors (Becque grudgingly admits he is using the term in its broadest sense) and artists. Professors "legislate" and pontificate and, despite their principles and their arrogance, are regularly proved wrong. The creative artist, on the other hand, is carried away by his enthusiasm, but what he admires and defends survives and merits survival.

Becque, moreover, does not confine his strictures to popular critics like Sarcey, Wolff, or Parigot. He is equally fearless in his opposition to the giants of his day–to Brunetière and to Taine–as well as to all those who, overlooking the individual merit of a work, judge it in the light of existing rules, personal prejudice, or preconceived ideas. Dogmatic criticism was anathema to Becque. Like Baudelaire and like his contemporary Jules Lemaître, he was opposed to "systems," to theories, to the belief that a work of art should comply with rules arbitrarily determined by the non-artist: "There are no theories. Theories are useless; they are confused; they are almost always made by a man in order to explain to you what talent he has or thinks he has. There are only works, and it is the author of those works who, in writing them, discovers the formula. The real manifesto of Victor Hugo was not the *Préface de Cromwell,* but rather his play *Hernani*" (VII, 37).

Becque scoffs at Brunetière's idea that the critic is charged with the responsibility of preserving literary tradition. On the contrary, he answers Brunetière, it is the creative artist "who produces it; it is he who maintains it; it is he who imposes it; you only record it twenty years later" (VI, 72). Becque is even more annoyed by Brunetière's "imperturbable assurance" in repudiating and condemning the rules which he had formerly defended and in replacing them with what he "somewhat majestically" called the "law." Like Baudelaire, Becque insists on the impossibility of finding a criterion applicable to every work of art: the criterion that will hold true in one case will only be disproved in another.

For much the same reasons, Becque objects to the dogmatic criticism of Taine who, he believed, was more concerned with proving his deterministic theories than with examining a work of art for itself. Taine's *Histoire de la littérature anglaise,* he observes, is ample evidence of the constant errors to which such a method leads. "Speak of the work itself, if you think you know it, and of the art which has produced it, if it is not altogether foreign to you," he admonishes the critic in an observation that echoes Flaubert's query: "Where do you know of any criticism that is deeply concerned with the work *itself?* The environment in which it is produced and the causes that brought it about are subtly analyzed. But the *unconscious* poetics? What explains them? Its composition, its style? the author's point of view? Never!"[1]

In a refreshing and original essay on Hamlet, Becque takes issue not only with Taine whose clinical eye viewed the prince of Denmark as the product of race, time, and milieu, but also with Goethe and the Romantic school who attempted to explain Hamlet's behavior by a state of mind bordering on insanity. Hamlet is of no century and of all centuries, he maintains. His contradictory qualities are the result of Shakespeare's substituting a man of revery for the man of action who is portrayed in the chronicle on which the tragedy is based. The murder of Polonius does not make Hamlet a man of the sixteenth century, as Taine and Montégut affirm, but is simply a borrowing from the original twelfth-century chronicle, which in turn recounts a tale of the eleventh century.

In his exasperation with the dogmatism practiced by university professors, Becque even lashes out against Aristotle, forgetting that it was Aristotle's commentators who were guilty of the dogmatism that he despised: "I have no patience with drama criticism, with Aristotle, first of all, and with his rules, his commentary, and his ignorance" (VI, 182). As for the rule of the unities, Becque dismisses it with obvious contempt, though elsewhere he admits a tendency on the part of his younger contemporaries to return to its use. Far from being a contradiction, Becque's observation was merely an expression of his belief that it is the artist who makes the rule.

An equally dangerous tendency of modern criticism, according to Becque, is the autobiographical approach which bases the interpretation of a work of art on the private life of the author. Critics, he maintains, confuse Alceste with Molière, and Hamlet with Shakespeare. "Nothing in the character and life of Molière authorizes this supposition, and the contrary supposition, [which Becque attempts to prove] would undoubtedly be more true" (VI, 168). Shakespeare, unlike the "lymphatic, asthmatic prince suffering from nerves" was "active, resolute, energetic, passionate." The author of innumerable love poems, he bore little resemblance to his Hamlet "who finds only four lines for Ophelia and stops there" (VI, 171, 172).

Professional criticism, according to Becque, is guilty not only of dogmatism but also of a tendency to be guided by personal tastes and prejudices. As a case in point, he singles out *L'Ecole des femmes (The School for Wives),* which he felt had been misinterpreted by well-meaning but misguided critics who attribute to its author their own personal preoccupations. Becque refuses to view Molière's famous play as a vehicle for the author's ideas on education and argues very convincingly that its theme is simply: "Love is the privilege of youth" (VII, 11). Had Molière been concerned with the problem of education, Becque adds, he would surely have made mention of that fact–either directly or indirectly–in his defense of his play, *La Critique de L'Ecole des femmes.* It was only critics of a later age who saw in the play the reflection of their own personal preoccupations.

The fault of most contemporary critics is the result of their failure to possess a certain "something" which has nothing to do with knowledge or formal training: "I have often wondered if education and learning were sufficient qualifications to judge a work of art and if it were not necessary to add something which cannot be learned." This "something," he goes on to ask "is it not a secret community of impressions, of feeling, and of dreams that exists between creator and critic?" (VI, 68-69). It is the lack of this very understanding that explains why theatrical works pass through three generations of professors: the first of which does not understand them, the second of which understands them badly, and the last of which understands them in a different way" (VI, 69).

II *Esthetic Ideas*

Basic to Becque's critical judgments are the esthetic ideas which determine his thinking. Presented unsystematically as a part of his critical analyses–whether in the form of reviews, articles, or lectures–they are more negative than positive in outlook, since, like Zola, he was primarily concerned with doing away with artificial restraints and with attaining the liberty for which Victor Hugo had once argued in the *Préface de Cromwell.*

Whereas the goal of art for Baudelaire and Flaubert had been beauty, for Becque it is truth. In order to arrive at the truth and to present an accurate picture of life, the artist must observe; he must paint only what he sees, for above all, his role is that of an observer. It is this emphasis on truth that mainly differentiates Becque from Baudelaire and Flaubert and places him squarely among the Realists.

To Baudelaire, even more than to Flaubert, imagination is "the queen of faculties." Of supreme importance to the artist, it is imagination, rather than observation, that aids him to conquer nature and to discover true Reality. Becque, on the other hand, says almost nothing about the imagination, and, when he alludes to it in passing, it is plain that he equates it with inventiveness, that he is far from thinking of it as a divine gift that helps the artist to penetrate the mysteries of life. In fact, Becque is too much the Realist to be concerned with the mysteries of life. It was in an interview with Tissot that his conception of the role of the imagination is made most clear: "An author always imagines something. That is inevitable. The important thing is that what he invents harmonizes with the rest and creates the same illusion. What is more, one can imagine the real, just as one can imagine the ideal."[2]

But if Becque is strictly a Realist in the importance he attaches to observation and truth, he stops short of Naturalism in his scorn for its scientific pretensions and its concern for documentation: "I don't copy. I have never taken a note. I make use of accumulated observations, gathered everywhere, without method and without purpose. . . .[3]

Freedom, a key word in Becque, is, however, absolutely essential:

A dramatist is free, absolutely free. He has no restrictions of any kind. He may vary his compositions in all sorts of ways; he may give them the ending that he wants or, if he wishes, he may not give them any at all. It will remain his secret. He is not obliged to take sides, to defend the pros and cons. He is only a spectator, a painter, a portrayer; his business is to hold up the mirror to Humanity. He will paint it as he wishes; he will idealize it, if he wishes—after all, to compose is really to idealize; he will even go so far as to create a myth or a symbol, but only on the condition of adhering to the truth and of not altering it. (VII, 105)

In other words, unlike the critic, the artist has a system—not one that is arbitrarily imposed on him by the critic but one that derives from his own individuality: "An artist's system is his stamp, his originality; it is the new element that he adds to what others have contributed. System is to be condemned only when it falls into the hands of sterile imitators who use it merely to mask their impotence" (V, 135-36).

It is through observation that the dramatist succeeds in achieving his principal function—that of creating character. Becque's insistence on the importance of character portrayal reveals more clearly than anything else the classical bent of his genius. Unlike most of his contemporaries, he views ideas as merely secondary in the hierarchy of values: "Ideas do not count for a dramatic author, it is only characters who count. Ideas are debatable and uncertain; they can be turned around; it is their application which gives them their value or their lack of value; characters, on the contrary, are invariable and absolute, and the function of a dramatist is not to discuss ephemeral ideas, but to paint eternal characters" (VII, 104).

Not that drama need be lacking in ideas or in the serious: "What is serious in the theater is not to be found in ideas. It is in the digestion of the ideas by the characters, in the dramatic or comic force which the characters give to the ideas" (VII, 76). Shakespeare does not discuss ideas, Becque affirms; "he makes of ideas a character, a man who represents them" (VII, 104).

Becque was especially opposed to the thesis play in which characters and situations serve only to prove the author's viewpoint. In fact, his intemperate attacks on both Dumas *fils* and Augier were provoked in large part by their predilection for the thesis play. "If he [the author] wishes to support an opinion, to defend a thesis, what is the result? He will portray problematical characters, extraordinary situations; he will arrive at only exceptional truths" (VI, 252).

In accusing Augier of "betraying his theater" by relying heavily on the "two old chestnuts of dramatic art: divorce and illegitimate children" (VII, 75), Becque seems to have forgotten that he too had been guilty of writing thesis plays and that he had been the first to demonstrate the need for a divorce law in his play *L'Enlèvement.* Despite his brief flirtation with the thesis drama, however, he remains adamantly opposed to it in theory and, as late as 1897, reaffirms his earlier judgment: "I despise thesis plays which are almost always poor plays and poor theses. I thought so in Dumas' day, and I have never changed my mind, far from it" (VII, 227).

Becque's dislike for thesis drama was in part related to his distaste for utilitarian art, for the moral preaching that had marked the works of the preceding generation. Like Baudelaire and Flaubert, he was strongly opposed to moral teaching both in dramatic and nondramatic art: "The theater is not meant to teach a moral lesson. The theater is a picture, a portrayal. Therein lies its purpose, its value, its very greatness" (VII, 40). When, as in the case of Victor Hugo, a moral lesson becomes the primary goal of the author, the work loses both in truth and in artistry.

Becque rather reluctantly admits, however, that morality may be implicit in art, that it may be a by-product rather than an end-product. "Of all the dramatic authors who have been true moralists, Molière is the greatest," he affirms (VII, 80). But the moralism of Molière, he maintains, has nothing in common with that of a Dumas *fils* or an Augier. His moralism, if such it can be called, was not a deliberate effort to teach a moral lesson but rather the result of "all the great manifestations of the mind and the disinterested knowledge of human affairs" that reveal themselves in his plays (VII, 24). For Molière was above all a dramatist who had little interest in ideas, in moral lessons, or in giving practical advice and "whose instinct, whose genius, whose function was to portray his fellowman" (VII, 23). In contrast, Diderot and Voltaire, who used the stage as a means of propagating their ideas and imposing their views on the public, had produced a theater that was long since dead.

In his admission that morality may be implicit in art, Becque again recalls the criticism of Baudelaire and Flaubert. But where he is loath to admit even an implicit morality, the author of *Les Fleurs du Mal* unhesitatingly declares that "every work of art that is *well done* naturally and necessarily suggests a moral."[4] Flaubert had expressed much the same idea in even more categorical terms: "If the reader doesn't draw from a book the morality which is to be found there, either the reader is an idiot or the book is false from the point of view of exactitude."[5] This difference of viewpoint, however, is not as great as it may appear. Were Baudelaire and Flaubert to have explained their conception of moralism, they might well have agreed with Becque that true morality lies in "all the great manifestations of the mind and the disinterested knowledge of human affairs."

Becque condemns not only all explicit moral comment but also any other form of personal intrusion in a work of art. His is not so much the scientific impersonality of the Naturalists, however, as the belief that impersonality is inherent in all great art and that the truly great creator is one who has the power to stand outside of himself:

> I am perfectly willing to accept the idea that an author observes himself and knows himself. I believe that his personal experiences can be useful to him. And I would even admit that a well-rounded author has in him the germ of all sentiments, good as well as bad, which he is called on to depict. But one cannot ask more of him. When it is a question of great creators like Shakespeare and Molière, "those fabricators of souls," as they have been called, it is to misunderstand them, to misunderstand their genius to make of them ordinary autobiographers. They are impersonal. I shall not say that this constitutes all their greatness, but it does constitute a good share of their greatness. (VI, 251)

As might be expected, Becque was strongly opposed to the cult of exterior form which characterized so much of the drama of his day. Though he himself was an able technician and though he admired the skillful construction of Sardou's plays and even, surprisingly enough, of *La Dame aux camélias*, he strongly objected to subordinating content to form: "I do not feel that craftsmanship, that craftsmanship which we talk about everyday, is the prime requisite and the chief merit in the theater" (VII, 89). Rules and conventions, whether those of the "well-made play" or of other types of drama are equally obnoxious: "I do not believe at all in what are called theatrical conventions, those conventions which are thrown in our faces and which, if they were not variable and changing, would make of dramatic art, as Monsieur Larroument has so aptly remarked, the most inflexible of arts" (VII, 90).

Drama should not be fitted into any particular mold or be required to follow a set pattern. To maintain, as did Dumas *fils* and Sarcey, that the theater is the art of preparation is to make theory out of one's talent: "When Dumas tells us: the theater is the art of preparation, that means: the theater of *Dumas* is the art of preparation. And one understands perfectly well that Dumas, who was always preoccupied in making the public swallow this, that or the other thing, needed more care and more preparation than anyone else" (VII, 89).

Becque was perfectly correct in his analysis of Dumas' technique. He himself was not unaware of the importance of preparation in order to give logic and verisimilitude to his dramas. But where Becque usually depends on characters to motivate his action, Dumas, like other writers of the "well-made play," often relies on a sort of artifical motivation whereby even the most accidental development in a drama is made to seem natural and logical, so subtly has the author managed to suggest its possibility.

Closely associated with Becque's belief that theatrical conventions are necessarily variable and changing is his conviction that drama, like all art, should bear "the stamp of its time," that it should be representative of the age in which it is produced. "All our originality comes from the stamp that time imprints on our feelings," Baudelaire had written many years earlier.[6] Becque was voicing much the same idea in maintaining that each period of art has its own "particular character" and that critics who avidly seek this "particular character" in the literature of the past ironically decry its presence in the literature of their own day.

Believing, as he did, in the freedom of the dramatist to determine form as well as content and recognizing the need for flexibility and change, Becque found himself unable to arrive at a definition of drama that would encompass all its possibilities: "If I were asked to define a play or if I were forced to concoct an aphorism, I would say: a play is an action, characters, and style. But that would just be another commonplace to add to so many others and would not lead to anything. The only thing I can say is that a play is recognized above all by this—that it is a composition which has a beginning, a middle, and an end" (VII, 90).

III *His Evaluation of Nineteenth-Century Drama—First Period*

Becque's criticism of the drama of the nineteenth century is revealing both in his appraisal of the authors that he discusses and in what it tells us about Becque himself. In a lecture on the theater of the nineteenth century, given in Milan on May 22, 1893, he divides the century into three periods. To the first he gives the name "period of imagination"—a term which he prefers to titles such as Romantic, historical, or revolutionary.

In spite of his tremendous admiration for Victor Hugo, whom he considers "the greatest lyric poet who has ever lived," comparable only to Homer, Milton, and Dante in poetic power, Becque has strong reservations about his theater. He recognizes Hugo's ability to construct a play, to exploit all the dramatic possibilities of a situation, and even to create "the most beautiful scenes with characters in whom we do not believe." But Hugo, he points out, was unfortunately given to moral teaching in his art—a fact which had also provoked the condemnation of Baudelaire many years earlier. Believing in the "civilizing mission" of the drama and obsessed by a fondness for antithesis, Hugo had composed all his plays according to a set pattern or "system." With his sense of pity and his "evangelical spirit," he constantly attempted to preach a moral lesson and to rehabilitate his characters, thereby destroying both the validity and freedom of the drama (VII, 37-41).

When Becque ranks Dumas *père* as "the great dramatic author of this period," it is important to note that he immediately adds by way of explanation: "He has scarcely any interest in teaching a moral lesson" (VII, 41). While admitting the fecundity and inventive genius of Dumas, Becque is clearly aware of his many faults. Dumas' unscrupulousness in borrowing from others, both in France and abroad, his use of paid collaborators, and his factory methods explain in large part the failure of his work to survive. "Mere trash," Jules Lemaître had once remarked on seeing a revival of *Henri III et sa cour,* and Becque repeats the remark with obvious approval. "Everything taken into account," Becque concludes, "he [Dumas] has left a great name, a work doomed to oblivion, and a fine heritage" (VII, 42).

Though Becque fails to mention Alfred de Vigny, in his lecture in Milan, he had written a review of *Chatterton* in 1877 and there is no reason to believe that he had changed his mind. The author of *Les Corbeaux* dismisses Vigny's drama as "elementary and insipid," objects to the constant sermonizing of the Quaker, and has praise only for the final scene in which Chatterton and Kitty Bell die, after confessing their love for each other. As for Chatterton himself, Becque agrees with Vigny that he belongs to the family of Hamlet, Werther, and René, but insists that he is too exaggerated to be of any real interest to the spectator (VI, 64-65).

In Becque's opinion, the comedy of the first period of the nineteenth century has "neither the dash, the verve, nor the daring of the drama" (VII, 42). The most successful of the writers of comedy, he suggests, was Scribe who was unquestionably a brilliant technician with a thorough knowledge of the theater. A writer of only average imagination, completely lacking style, "a superficial and hasty observer who was never deeply troubled by the spectacle of the world," Scribe never forced his talent and was content "to amuse and to make us smile"(VII, 44).

Of all the writers of the first period, Becque admires none more sincerely than Alfred de Musset. He has only the warmest praise for Musset's theater, "half real and half dream" with its mingling of passion, observation, sensibility, wit, and fantasy. Like Zola, he especially admires *On ne badine pas avec l'amour* and *Le Chandelier* and has no hesitation in characterizing his plays as "exquisite."

Musset's discovery of new and bold subjects, his ability to execute them with a sure hand, his knowledge of feminine psychology, and his use of "an admirable language, the old French language renewed and revitalized by a romantic inspiration" set him apart from his contemporaries, according to Becque, and make him "the most skillful of dramatic writers" (VII, 45). "It would be very amusing," Becque adds, "if Alfred de Musset were the only dramatist of the century to survive, especially since he never considered himself a dramatist and since that title had been denied him by the Parisian criticism of his day." Becque may have been alluding to Sainte-Beuve, who failed to recognize the originality of Musset's theater and who saw in *Il ne faut jurer de rien (You Can Never be Sure)* a loosely constructed play, lacking good sense and containing "many pretty things."[7]

It is to Becque's credit that, despite the great disparity between his genius and that of Musset, he was able to appreciate the delicate art of the Romantic poet. He would have found it even more amusing had he known that, of all the French dramatists of the nineteenth century, he himself and Musset were to be hailed as the greatest of their time. "N'est-ce pas que c'est drôle?" he might well have remarked to his friends with his usual hearty laugh.

IV *Nineteenth-Century Drama–Second Period*

To the second period of nineteenth-century drama beginning with *La Dame aux camélias* in 1852 and usually known as Realism, Becque gives the name "period of wit." In many ways, his choice of title is preferable to that used by literary historians, for the drama of the period is too artificial both in plot and character to be considered truly realistic. On the other hand, the witty dialogue and constant irony in which it abounds amply justify Becque's description.

In addition to Augier, Dumas *fils,* and Sardou–the three best known representatives of the period–Becque singles out Labiche and two sets of collaborators: Meilhac and Halévy, and Pailleron and Gondinet. George Sand, Jules Sandeau, and Octave Feuillet are mentioned only in passing, since, as Becque reminds his audience, they had been somewhat undeservedly forgotten by the public.

Becque's criticism of Emile Augier is a little disappointing. He overrates his verse drama, even while admitting Augier's inadequacies as a poet, and somewhat underestimates his prose drama. Augier's resemblance to Molière is in Becque's opinion a misconception: "Molière is always a comic author, and Augier is never one" (VII, 47). On the contrary, Becque maintains, Augier seems to have derived his moral eloquence from Corneille, his inventions from Regnard, and his mannered tendencies from Marivaux.

Moreover, unlike Molière, Augier creates characters that are "confused, colorless, and incomplete; one doen't see them." His description, though true enough in many cases, seems hardly applicable to Monsieur Poirier or to Maître Guérin, both of whom Becque fails to mention. Augier's system, Becque maintains, is invariably the same: a meaningless title, several arbitrary intrigues, and an uninteresting marriage as a conclusion. The result in each case is a brilliant but artificial composition. Augier's real merit, Becque concludes, lies in his "firm and elegant–sometimes too elegant–style," in his wit, and in the strong moral impression left by his works (VII, 49).

Both in his lecture in Milan as well as elsewhere in his criticism, Becque shows himself especially severe in his judgment of Dumas *fils.* It is true that his dislike of Dumas' theater was intensified by the personal animosity which he felt for his popular rival. He could not easily forget that Dumas opposed his acceptance into the French Academy and had voted against awarding the *prix Montyon* to *Les Corbeaux.*[8]

Yet even under different circumstances Becque's criticism would doubtless have been equally severe, for he was deeply opposed to Dumas' utilitarian conception of the theater–to his use of the drama as a vehicle for moral teaching rather than for the portrayal of character: "Dumas thought that the theater was a means of instruction and that it was more noble to propagate ideas than to create characters" (VII, 52).

Instead of becoming "the painter of his day, the complete painter of all society," Dumas chose to prove a thesis with the help of a *raisonneur.* As a consequence, his characters are mere puppets: "All these brilliant creatures, it must be admitted, are marionnettes in the hands of Dumas. He thinks and he speaks for them; he conducts them as he wishes. He started with one idea in imagining them and they serve only to prove his demonstrations" (VII, 55).

Becque sincerely admires *La Dame aux camélias*, which he considers well constructed, though badly written. He likewise admires *Le Demi-Monde* in spite of its artificiality and its unduly complicated intrigue of which he is not unaware. The rest of Dumas' theater, Becque complains, deals repeatedly with the same themes and with the same characters: the bewildered and determined woman of good society at odds with her husband, her guilty husband "stupid, idle, and libertine," the man she loves–a sort of Father Joseph who confesses, catechizes, and saves his victims–and finally the young girl who has been seduced.

The latter, Becque declares, had become a veritable obsession with Dumas. He has portrayed her in every possible situation: when her lover marries her; when her lover does not marry her; when she marries someone else and acknowledges her child; when she marries someone else and hides her child; and finally when she marries someone else and her child is dead. The only situation Dumas has failed to exploit, Becque drily remarks, is when the young girl has several children and marries "someone else" (VII, 55).

While justifying the young girl in question and pardoning her fault, Dumas also delights in portraying a sort of "repressed Don Juan without the weaknesses of his sex," who is adored by all women but remains impervious to their charms. The final impression left on the reader by this attempt to present a moral lesson is a strange one, Becque concludes. Evidently "Dumas wanted to transfer virginity–to impose it on men and no longer require it of women" (VII, 56).

It is often claimed that Becque's praise of Sardou was as much motivated by personal prejudice as were his attacks on Dumas *fils*, for it can hardly be denied that Sardou's plays are as artificial in construction and character portrayal as those of his contemporary. Becque was deeply grateful for the kindness and encouragement shown him by Sardou early in his career, and it seems fairly obvious that, consciously or unconsciously, he sought to minimize the faults and to stress the merits of his theater. He rightly acknowledges Sardou's dramatic sense, his versatility, and his knowledge of his craft. Above all, he approves the fact that his plays were written to be plays rather than sermons and that they are concerned with characters rather than ideas.

On the other hand, Becque seems perfectly aware of Sardou's melodramatic tendencies and almost overly anxious to excuse them: "He knows all the resources of his art and, if he misuses them sometimes, at least it is not to make us swallow this or that; he only wishes to add a little inventiveness, fantasy, and surprise to the representation of reality" (VII, 56). Elsewhere there is no mistaking Becque's mild rebuke in speaking of Sardou's comedy *Odette:* "If the artist in Monsieur Sardou is sometimes at fault, the creator is always admirable" (V, III).

Somewhat surprisingly, Becque compares Sardou to Balzac, especially in the more melodramatic aspects of their work. He cites not only the powerful imagination, the feverish work, and the fertility in conception that characterize the two writers, but he also points out the more sensational aspects of their work: "Both are preoccupied by mysteries, conspiracies, and the police. They believed in magnetism, in spiritism; they are suspicious of suggestion. These two minds are very similar, all-conquering and visionary" (VII, 57).

With the exception of Augier, Dumas *fils,* and Sardou, most of the writers belonging to the "period of wit" are in Becque's opinion artists "doubling as manufacturers." The "firm of Meilhac and Halévy," who specialized in witty operettas, witty vaudevilles, and witty comedies, seem to him the most brilliant and fruitful of all the collaborators. Their "trademark," like that of their competitors, is a subtle irony which had become very fashionable. To Meilhac and Halévy, as well as to all the members of the "I-don't-give-a-hang" school who indiscriminately make light of everything, irony had come to replace the bitterness *(amertume)* which Sainte-Beuve once maintained gives force its savor. The only drawback to such an approach is, in Becque's opinion, the difficulty of maintaining the irony throughout an entire play, especially in the face of passion, suffering, and death. Although no collaboration had proved more fruitful and brilliant than that of Halévy and Meilhac, all their plays seem to Becque to have something improvised and unfinished about them and never quite succeed in becoming true works of art.

Becque is even more caustic in speaking of Pailleron, whose poetry and plays he dismisses as completely mediocre. *Le Monde où l'on s'ennuie (The Boring Society)* seems to him brilliant and amusing, though somewhat flawed by the author's inability to successfully portray the principal character. Gondinet, the collaborator of Pailleron, though equal in talent to his partner and possessing far more verve, invention, and fecundity, had, in Becque's opinion, allowed himself to be used and had died without leaving a work worthy of his ability.

Becque's hostile judgment of Labiche was strongly motivated by sympathy for his collaborators who, he believed, had contributed so greatly to the success of the popular playwright without receiving the recognition that they deserved. Becque could not forget that one of the forgotten collaborators had been his uncle Martin Lubize, whose contribution to *Le Misanthrope et l'Auvergnat* had gone almost unrecognized.

Becque argues that the most successful plays of Labiche were those written in collaboration with Marc-Michel, Delacour, and Edouard Martin, each of whom had left an indelible stamp upon the works in question. On the other hand, he maintains that the poorest plays were those written either alone or together with Raymond Deslandes.

Becque's distaste for Labiche was further increased by the latter's financial success and by the ecstatic praise of university critics who sought to disprove their own lack of wit and humor by hailing the dramatist as "an artist in gaiety, a philosopher of gaiety" (VII, 60). Showing some of the same irascibility that marks his attitude to Dumas *fils,* the author of *La Parisienne* characterizes the comedies of Labiche as "vacuous and meaningless" and wrongly contends that his work had become "intolerable and unreadable" to the present generation.

V *Nineteenth-Century Drama–Period of Truth*

The third and last period into which Becque divides nineteenth-century drama begins with *Les Corbeaux* (1882) and is called by him "the period of truth." Unlike the theater of the preceding generation, it rejects the moralism and preaching which had marred so much of the work of Augier and Dumas and relies entirely on observation. "I am going to indicate the great difference that exists between the writers of today and yesterday," Becque states categorically in a lecture given in Marseilles in 1895. "From this difference stems all the rest: our predecessors were moralists, and we are observers" (VII, 79).

The young writers of the day–about twenty in number–have turned their backs on the past, he explains in a lecture given two years earlier, and are concerned only with portraying life as it is. To achieve their goal, they have not hesitated to abandon the successful formulas of their predecessors. They have dispensed with the plot that invariably ends with a happy marriage, they have dispensed with the likable character who arouses admiration and with the witty person so eagerly awaited by the spectators. They have, in fact, dispensed with all arbitrary characters and situations and seek only the representation of life and truth.

By thus rejecting the artificiality and banality of contemporary drama, by minimizing and even suppressing action, and by emphasizing careful character analysis, they are in reality returning to "the great theater, the classic theater." They have rediscovered the same form of art, the same *procédés;* in many cases they have even returned, though unconsciously, to the rule of the three unities.

It was André Antoine, Becque maintains, who had saved dramatic art by opening the doors of the Théâtre-Libre to these dedicated young writers who until then had been ignored by ultraconservative directors and critics. Thanks to the efforts of Antoine, a brilliant actor as well as a successful producer, the new drama was beginning to find a place for itself. Even criticism was beginning to undergo a change and was becoming more receptive to new ideas. Becque's allusion to certain discriminating minds *(esprits fins)* among the critics is undoubtedly a reference to Henry Bauër, Louis Ganderax, and Jules Lemaître, who were among those who had shown themselves most sympathetic to the new school of drama. Bauër had become one of the most fanatical partisans of the Naturalistic school, while Lemaître, famous for his brilliant, impressionistic articles, was somewhat more eclectic in his tastes.

Far from aiding the cause of the new school of dramatists, the Naturalists had actually proved to be "most dangerous allies." Becque does not hesitate to condemn what he considers the crudeness and vulgarity of their literature: "Naturalism, it must be said, has resorted to impressive words to excuse and protect itself: psychology, physiology, scientific observation substituted for moral analyses and entertaining representation. In plain French, it has shown a liking for filth, filth of all kinds—that of men, of actions, and of words" (VI, 109).

Although Becque, like Flaubert, acknowledges the sweeping power of Zola's novels, he strongly dislikes his choice of characters and situations. "I have little taste for murderers, neurasthenics, alcoholics, for the martyrs of heredity and the victims of evolution," he writes in his preface to *Les Corbeaux* (II, 339). Becque may have been thinking in particular of *L'Assommoir (The Dram Shop),* which Busnach and Gastineau had adapted for the stage in 1879. An out-and-out melodrama, *L'Assommoir* had had a long run at the Ambigu, where the famous scene depicting Coupeau suffering from delirium tremens had attracted large crowds of curious spectators.

Becque was even more disgusted by the attempt of the Naturalistic novelists to reform the theater: "All these gentlemen—Goncourt, Flaubert, Zola—had promised to revolutionize the theater. They produced magnificent theories and very mediocre works. Directors didn't fail to tell us: there you see, that's what the new school produces" (VII, 63-64). If *Henriette Maréchal* of the Goncourts, *Le Candidat* of Flaubert, and *Bouton de Rose (Rose Bud)* of Zola had met with ignominious failure, it was largely, Becque affirms, because their authors lacked the gift necessary for the creation of successful drama and because they considered drama an art secondary in importance to the novel. Fortunately, the decay of the theater, which had begun with *Henriette Maréchal*, had been arrested by Antoine whose discovery of vigorous young talent like that of Curel, Lavedan, and Brieux, had given new life to the theater.

Despite his allegiance to the new school, Becque was quite aware of its faults: "I know very well, Ladies and Gentlemen, the reproach that can be made my friends and, more than once, I myself have warned them of it in private. They were faced with a danger and they have not avoided it. That danger is cynicism" (VII, 66). Blaming the excesses of the school on the pernicious influence of the art and literature of the day, he looks hopefully to the future: "Before long, when they are more sure of their method and when their field of observation has been enlarged, we shall have a theater which will differ very sharply from preceding theaters, which will no doubt be superior to them and which, from now on, may be called the period of truth" (VII, 66).

Five years later, in 1898, writing to the Belgian author, Georges Rodenbach, who had just published an article on the contemporary theater, Becque still finds it necessary to apologize for the faults of his disciples: "I notice .... a little severity on your part for my neighbors of the *comédie rosse.* Their great mistake has been to confine themselves to somewhat low milieux and to characters who are too mediocre. But they were returning to the theater of the seventeenth century, where the subject was treated—the whole subject, nothing but the subject—with that simplification of events that you have so correctly noted" (VII, 222).

Under the circumstances, it is quite understandable that Becque should be both pleased and somewhat perturbed at the thought that the new school had adopted him as their leader. Even though he had written no plays for the Théâtre-Libre—for which he had been publicly chided by Céard—Antoine considered Becque "the true renovator of the contemporary theater" and in his *Souvenirs* affectionately calls him "the real master and leader of the whole new movement." Other members of Antoine's entourage were equally enthusiastic and loyal.

Becque, who had known so little praise and acclaim in his life, was touched but somewhat ill at ease. If he was acknowledged as the head of the school, he told his audience in 1893, it was largely because he was the oldest of the group. In reality, he added, the new movement had begun with his friends rather than with himself (VII, 62). Two years later, at a lecture given in Marseilles on November 27, 1895, he seemed even more conscious of the gap between him and his young disciples: "I have found myself placed between two generations of dramatic authors, like the character of La Fontaine between two mistresses–one who wanted to snatch out my black hair, the other who didn't see my white hair. Well, Ladies and Gentlemen, I prefer the second mistress" (VII, 83).

CHAPTER 8

Conclusion

Becque—Naturalist or Classicist?

BECQUE had every reason to feel somewhat apart from his would-be followers, for, with the exception of the unfinished *Les Polichinelles,* there was a world of difference between his dramas and the typical *comédie rosse* being performed at the Théâtre-Libre. Jules Lemaître was one of the first to note the differences and to insist that Becque was free from the disagreeable exaggerations of his young disciples. Writing in 1888, after seeing *La Parisienne* played by Réjane and Antoine in the salon of Madame Aubernon, he takes pains to distinguish it from the "brutal literature" of young men who, he claims, "are plainly imitating Monsieur Becque:" "I beg you, first of all, not to confuse it *[La Parisienne]* with the lugubrious 'hoaxes' of the Théâtre-Libre."[1]

Like La Rochefoucauld, La Bruyère, Chamfort, and almost all moralists and comic authors, Lemaître adds, Becque finds "a delicious intellectual pleasure" in noting the most lamentable aspects of reality. The writers of the Théâtre-Libre, on the other hand, experience a "superb joy" in their scorn for mankind and for life. They take an almost voluptuous pleasure in portraying "the fatalities of the flesh, the brutalities of the instincts." Unlike them, Becque is a "jovial" pessimist, "a misanthrope laughing heartily, [who] decries the universe while holding his sides."[2] He is ferocious with impartiality and out of pure love for his art. He derives so much artistic pleasure from his cruelest words that he robs them of their bitterness.

Though Lemaître's comments apply mainly to *La Parisienne,* he felt just as strongly about *Les Corbeaux.* After seeing the revival of Becque's earlier masterpiece at the Odéon in 1897, he reiterates the views he had expressed nine years before: "Monsieur Becque is free from the prejudices and the unpleasant exaggerations by which his young disciples were to distinguish themselves easily and noisily. He doesn't indulge in puerile pessimism, in amateur Schopenhauerism; and in general he avoids what Monsieur Francisque Sarcey once unhesitatingly called the 'genre rosse.'—His decent people are victims, because that's the way things go in the world; but at least he believes that decent people exist. And he loves them."[3]

Like Henry Bauër, Lemaître sees in Becque's plays a return to classic comedy and to the art of Molière. In *La Parisienne* he had been struck by the author's resemblance to Molière in inventing telling phrases that characterize the speaker or the situation. In *Les Corbeaux* he notes the classic manner of his construction and character portrayal: "Monsieur Henry Becque, with admirable determination, is restoring the great realistic comedy which doubtless was not absent from the work of his predecessors, but which failed to show itself, if one may say so, in its pure state: listen to a play in which (just as in a tragedy of Racine, of all things) the initial situation is engendered by the characters and is then developed with all possible smoothness and without any intrusion of chance."[4]

Gustave Kahn, writing in the *Revue Blanche* in 1899, the year of Becque's death, corroborates this judgment and maintains that the author of *Les Corbeaux* was "a classicist to the very tips of his fingers. He even had their idiosyncracies," he adds,—"he dispatched the epistle just as coolly and the epigram just as briskly as the masters of the genre."[5]

That same year Jules Wogue, in an article in the *Grande Revue,* expressed much the same opinion. "The immense merit of Becque," he affirms, "was not to be a precursor, not to orient comedy in new directions, but to bring it back to its former bourgeois and classic conception."[6]

Auguste Filon, on the other hand, while noting Becque's resemblance to Molière in his portrayal of characters, does not hesitate to characterize both *Les Corbeaux* and *La Parisienne* as *comédies rosses.* If, as he maintains, "rosserie" is a sort of "vicious ingenuousness," a "childlike and paradisiac tranquility in corruption," he is undoubtedly right.[7] Becque's infamous characters seem completely unaware of their turpitude; their impeccable manners and speech only accentuate their unprincipled actions. Filon's viewpoint was more or less typical of the critical thought of his day, for, as Martino points out, around 1890 Becque was generally considered "the father of the *comédie rosse,* the last and most perfect incarnation of the Naturalistic theater."[8]

The question of Becque's relationship to Naturalism continues to be a subject of debate even today. While most authors of manuals and histories of literature consider him the father of Naturalistic drama, others, like Dumesnil, maintain that nothing was further from the truth, that Becque was never a Naturalist, and that the great error of his contemporaries was to see in him a disciple of Zola.[9] Most biographers of Becque tend to be of the same opinion. In his monograph of 1930, Paul Blanchart sees in the author of *Les Corbeaux* "an authentic classicist, a strict disciple of Molière, and a direct descendant of Marivaux and of Regnard."[10] He was not the first Realist, Blanchart states categorically, "he is precisely the last Classicist. Let us add: one of the most pure, the most admirable among our Classicists."[11]

Arnaoutovitch, the author of a three-volume study of Becque and his work, sees in the dramatist a revolutionary formed in the tradition of three centuries, the unconscious continuer of Molière, who, strongly influenced by Balzac, successfully overthrew the artificial drama of the day and became the most important representative of the true and Realistic theater of the nineteenth century.

The author of the most recent monograph on Becque, Maurice Descotes, likewise concludes that Becque owes something to a long tradition going back to Molière of the seventeenth century and to the ideas of realistic drama formulated by Diderot in the eighteenth century. Descotes views Becque as an independent, belonging to no particular school, who allowed himself to be presented as a precursor and protector of the Théâtre-Libre, even though his influence on the members of the group was only minimal.

In a certain sense, all these judgments are more or less valid. There is no doubt that, in the creation of character, Becque is often reminiscent of Molière and that he created eternal types worthy of the great seventeenth-century dramatist. There is no doubt also that Antoine and the members of the Théâtre-Libre looked to Becque as their guide and mentor, for they found in him an ideal of naturalness and simplicity which had been almost completely absent from the theater of Augier and Dumas *fils.* Because he was conscious of the attempt of his young contemporaries to simplify action and to stress character analysis, Becque, as we have seen, tended to overemphasize the fact that the new movement was "a return to the great theater, to the classic theater:" "We are re-discovering the same form of art and the same *procédés:* simple action–one might say almost no action at all; minute and imperturbable analysis; situations and characters that are repeated to the point of exhaustion. And the resemblances do not stop there. There is still another, one that is very strange and that should disarm traditional criticism. Unintentionally and almost unknowingly, there is a return to the rule of the three unities" (VII, 65-66).

Becque's observations may explain why Jules Lemaître, despite his insistence on the differences between Becque's theater and that of the new school, could still write in 1897: "It has often been noticed, and quite rightly, that the whole Théâtre-Libre derives from *Les Corbeaux.*" And why he firmly maintained: "*Les Corbeaux* . . . will mark a date in the history of our theater, the first important date since that of *La Dame aux camélias.*"[12]

The fact is that Becque himself contributed nothing to the Théâtre-Libre and had virtually ceased to produce when Antoine first established his theater in 1887. It was his daring break with the conventional theater, the simplicity of his action, his use of the "slice of life" in *La Parisienne,* and his greater emphasis on characterization that appealed to the writers of the Théâtre-Libre and caused them to look upon him as their leader. But despite their admiration, they tended to follow–perhaps unconsciously–the example of the Naturalistic novelists in their emphasis on what Lemaître had called "the fatalities of the flesh, the brutalities of the instincts." Theirs was a more violent, more crude approach marked by all the excesses that characterize Naturalism at its worst. None succeeded in equaling the moving power of *Les Corbeaux* or the corrosive but civilized satire of *La Parisienne.*

In many ways, Becque's position may be likened to that of Flaubert. The author of *Madame Bovary* detested the label of Realist or Naturalist and refused to be categorized as such. Yet he is known to have been "the critical and paternal friend" as well as the "benevolent counselor" of both Realists and Naturalists and to have succeeded far better than Champfleury or Duranty in creating what has long been recognized as a masterpiece among Realistic novels.

Becque, likewise, scorned the Naturalists and sharply criticized their cynicism and their fondness for filth. Yet, like Flaubert, he was a close friend and confidant of the young writers whose very excesses were largely inspired by the literature he excoriated. Like Flaubert also, he dealt with middle-class characters rather than with the proletariat and avoided the crudity of manners and speech that so often characterized Naturalistic literature. Becque's situations were ignoble without being sordid, his vultures and amoralists un-regenerate without being bestial, his dialogue natural without being coarse.

Moreover, Becque's own statements would seem to deny any close affiliation with the Naturalists, for in his last lectures, as we have seen, he maintains that, if he was acknowledged the leader of the new school, it was only because of his age and that it was really his friends who had founded the new movement. Moreover, from the standpoint of chronology alone, Becque seems isolated from the Naturalists. If he wrote *Les Corbeaux* as early as 1872, which seems quite possible, or even in 1876, his theater antedates Zola's serious drama, and his originality becomes all the more obvious. Of even greater importance, his frank distaste for the application of scientific theories to literature, his scorn for what he called the "filth" of the Naturalists, his amused contempt for "documentation" ("I don't copy, I have never taken a note"), all reveal a marked disparity between his dramatic practice and the Naturalistic doctrine.

Becque's contribution to nineteenth-century drama lay, above all, in the naturalness of his technique and in his emphasis on truth and observation. In the formulation of his method, he had undoubtedly utilized some of the technical devices found in the Naturalistic novel, but even more he had absorbed and assimilated the ideas of bourgeois drama that had first been propagated by Diderot in the eighteenth century. The theater of Augier and Dumas *fils* had been realistic only in contrast to that of their predecessors–in their use of contemporary characters and contemporary problems. The artificial plot construction, the slick characterizations, the abundance of rhetoric and wit that stamp their plays resulted in a surface realism that is far from the unadulterated truth of Becque's drama. It is said that the theater in France is always the last stronghold to yield to innovations and that, in breaking with tradition, it lags ten to twenty years behind other literary genres. It is not surprising then that it was Becque, rather than Augier or Dumas *fils,* who finally succeeded in creating drama that seemed made of the very stuff of life itself.

But even more than a Realist firmly entrenched in the nineteenth century, Becque is a traditionalist whose roots go deep into the past and whose knowledge of the human heart and mind links him with the great writers of other centuries. Though his vision of life was too restricted to earn him a place among the truly great, he will always occupy an important place in the history of the French theater. Not only did he succeed in banishing the absurdities of the "well-made play" and in giving a new direction to French drama, but his two great masterpieces will remain as models of an uncompromising art that creates rather than imitates the reality from which it is derived.

Notes and References

Chapter One

1. References to Becque's works and to Robaglia's prefatory essay are to the seven-volume *Oeuvres complètes* (Crès, 1924-26).
2. Claude Roy, *Stendhal par lui-même* (Paris, 1954), p. 34.
3. Francisque Sarcey, "Chronique Théâtrale," *Le Temps* (November 9, 1868).
4. Marvin A. Carlson, *André Antoine's "Memories of the Théâtre-Libre"* (Coral Gables, Florida, 1964), p. 220.
5. Robert de Flers, *Deux hommages: Ronsard, Becque* (Paris, 1924), p. 27.
6. *Ibid.*, p. 29.
7. *Ibid.*, p. 32.
8. Edmond Sée, *Henry Becque ou Servitude et Grandeur dramatiques* (Paris, 1926), p. 53.
9. Gérard Bauër, "*La Parisienne* et Henry Becque," *Conférencia* (November, 1949), p. 470.

Chapter Two

1. In modern editions of *La Cagnotte* the songs have been omitted.
2. Paul Blanchart, *Henry Becque* (Paris, 1930), p. 43.

Chapter Three

1. Edmond Sée, *Henry Becque* (Paris, 1926), p. 36.
2. James Huneker, *Iconoclasts* (New York, 1919), p. 176.

Chapter Four

1. P. V. Stock, "Le Mémorandum d'un éditeur: Henry Becque anecdotique," *Mercure de France,* February 15, 1935, pp. 47-52.

Becque does not mention Stock's role in his account of the play nor the fact that, after the acceptance of *Les Corbeaux* by the Comédie, he contracted with Stock for a better price. Consequently, Robaglia, in his preface to the *Oeuvres complètes,* believes that Becque erred in saying that *Les Corbeaux* had been accepted at the Comédie-Française before it was printed.

2. See Emile Bouvier, "La Date de composition des *Corbeaux,*" *Revue d'Histoire littéraire de la France,* January-March, 1924, pp. 118-25.

3. Edmond Sée, *Henry Becque* (Paris, 1926), p. 35.

4. *Ibid.,* p. 38.

5. Louis Ganderax, "Revue dramatique: *Les Corbeaux,*" *Revue des Deux Mondes* (October 1, 1882), pp. 694-706.

6. Paul Hervieu, "Pessimisme et Comédie," *La Revue de Paris* (April, 1900), p. 737.

7. Ambroise Got, *Henry Becque* (Paris, 1920), p. 68.

Chapter Five

1. Robaglia in his preface to the *Oeuvres Complètes* is mistaken in his statement that the committee was unanimous in its opposition.

2. Gérard Bauër, "*La Parisienne* de Henry Becque," *Conférencia* (November, 1949), p. 463.

3. Antoine, *op. cit.* (Chap. 1, note 4, above), pp. 68-69.

4. Bauër, p. 468. According to Bauër, Becque had first thought of calling his play *Le Jaloux (The Jealous One).*

5. Bauër, p. 470.

6. Blanchart, *op. cit.* (Chap. 2, note 2, above), p. 55.

7. Bauër, p. 463.

8. Alexandre Arnaoutovitch, *Henry Becque* (Paris, 1927), Vol. III, p. 80.

9. *Ibid.,* p. 87.

10. Maurice Descotes, *Henry Becque et son théâtre* (Paris, 1962), p. 151.

11. Arnaoutovitch, Vol. I, pp. 531-34.

12. Jules Lemaître, *Impressions de Théâtre* (Paris, 1888-98), Vol. III, p. 226.

13. Arnaoutovitch, Vol. I, p. 487.

14. Lemaître, p. 230.

Chapter Seven

1. Gustave Flaubert, *Correspondance: Nouvelle Edition Augmentée,* Conard ed. (Paris, 1926-33), Vol. VI, p. 8.
2. Ernest Tissot, "Le Théâtre d'Henry Becque," *La Revue Générale,* (December, 1904), pp. 839-59.
3. *Ibid.*
4. Charles Baudelaire, *Correspondance Générale,* Conard ed. (Paris, 1947-53), Vol. IV, p. 198. Letter to Swinburne.
5. Flaubert, *Correspondance,* Vol. III, p. 344.
6. Baudelaire, *L'Art Romantique,* Conard ed. (Paris, 1925), p. 69.
7. Sainte-Beuve, *Mes Poisons* (Paris, 1926), p. 103.
8. A prize awarded by the French government for successful moralizing plays "designed for the instruction of the working classes through the propagation of healthy ideas and the spectacle of good examples."

Chapter Eight

1. Lemaître, Vol. III, p. 219.
2. *Ibid.,* pp. 221-22.
3. Lemaître, Vol. X, pp. 304-5.
4. *Ibid.,* p. 304.
5. Gustave Kahn, "Henry Becque," *La Revue Blanche,* 1899, Vol. XIX, p. 183.
6. Jules Wogue, "Le Théâtre de Henry Becque," *La Grande Revue,* 1899, Vol. IX, p. 606.
7. Auguste Filon, *De Dumas à Rostand* (Paris, 1898), p. 70.
8. Pierre Martino, *Le Naturalisme français* (Paris, 1923), p. 182.
9. René Dumesnil, *Le Réalisme et le Naturalisme* (Paris, 1955), p. 425.
10. Blanchart, p. 94.
11. *Ibid.,* p. 10.
12. Lemaître, Vol. X, pp. 303, 304.

Selected Bibliography

PRIMARY SOURCES

Original Editions

Sardanapale. Paris: Michel-Lévy frères, 1867.

L'Enfant prodigue. Paris: Michel-Lévy frères, 1868.

Michel Pauper. Paris: A. Lacroix, Verboeckhoven et Cie, 1871.

La Navette. Paris: Tresse, 1878.

Les Honnêtes Femmes. Paris: Tresse, 1880.

Les Corbeaux. Paris: Tresse, 1882.

Le Frisson, rhymed fantasy. Paris: Tresse.

La Parisienne. Paris: Calmann-Lévy, 1885.

Molière et l'Ecole des femmes, lecture. Paris: Tresse et Stock, 1886.

Sonnets mélancoliques. Brussels: Librairie nouvelle, 1887-88.

Querelles littéraires. Paris: E. Dentu, 1890.

Souvenirs d'un auteur dramatique. Paris: Bibliothèque artistique et littéraire, 1895.

Madeleine. Paris: *La Vie Parisienne,* June 27, 1896.

Veuve! Paris: *La Vie Parisienne,* January 23, 1897.

Le Domino à quatre. Paris: *La Vie Parisienne,* March 20, 1897.

Le Départ. Paris: *Revue de Paris,* May 1, 1897.

L'Enlèvement. Paris: *Revue du Palais,* May 1, 1897.

Une Exécution. Paris: *La Vie Parisienne,* July 24, 1897.

Les Polichinelles. [Complete reproduction of the unfinished manuscript]. Paris: *L'Illustration Théâtrale,* October 8, 1910.

Editions

Théâtre complet. 2 vols. Paris: G. Charpentier, 1890. Republished in 1910 and in 1916 under editorship of Eugène Fasquelle.

Théâtre complet. Paris: Bibliothèque artistique et littéraire, 1898, 3 vols. Known as La Plume edition.

Oeuvres complètes. 7 vols. Paris: Crès, 1924-26. With a preface by Jean Robaglia, the grandnephew of Becque. The most satisfactory edition of Becque's works, it contains much unpublished material including poems, lectures, and letters.

Translations

1. *The Crows.* Trans. Benedict Papot. *The Drama,* February, 1912, 14-126.

2. *The Vultures, The Woman of Paris, The Merry-Go-Round.* Trans. with an introduction by Freeman Tilden. New York, 1913.

3. *A Quiet Game (Le Domino à Quatre).* Trans. Sheba Harris. Play Book, Madison, Wis., 1913.

4. *The Shuttle.* Trans. L. A. Loiseau. New York. No date.

5. *The Vultures.* Trans. Freeman Tilden. In *Representative Continental Drama.* Ed. by Moses. Boston, 1924.

6. *Woman of Paris.* Trans. Jacques Barzun. *The Modern Theater,* 5 plays, ed. by Eric Bentley, Vol. I. Garden City, Doubleday and Co., 1955.

SECONDARY SOURCES

Biographies and Critical Studies

ARNAOUTOVITCH, ALEXANDRE. *Henry Becque.* 3 vols. Paris: Presses Universitaires de France, 1927. The definitive work on Becque containing a magnificent bibliography, especially of contemporary reviews. A doctoral thesis, its fragmented organization makes it very difficult to use. Tends to be too adulatory even of Becque's minor works.

BLANCHART, PAUL. *Henry Becque.* Paris: Nouvelle Revue critique, 1930. A brief (112 pages) but useful discussion of Becque's work. Devotes an entire chapter to Becque as a journalist, but only touches on his esthetic ideas.

DAWSON, ERIC. *Henry Becque, sa vie et son théâtre.* Paris: Payot, 1923. A doctoral thesis refused by the Sorbonne. The rejection of the thesis became a *cause célèbre* and was the subject of much discussion in the press. Becque's admirers saw it as further proof of the continued indifference of university professors to Becque's theater. A useful book but somewhat superficial and marred by a number of factual errors.

DESCOTES, MAURICE. *Henry Becque et son Théâtre.* Paris: M. J. Minard, 1962. The best and most useful book on Becque. Sees Becque as a man of the theater, independent of literary schools. Presents interesting material on the theaters of the day.

GOT, AMBROISE. *Henry Becque, sa vie et son oeuvre.* Paris: Crès, 1920. A doctoral thesis submitted at the University of Zurich. Contains a great many factual errors and over-emphasizes Becque's cynicism.

SÉE, EDMOND. *Henry Becque ou Servitude et grandeur dramatiques.* Paris: V. Rasmussen, 1926. A condensed résumé of material which Sée had already published in the form of articles. A eulogy of Becque rather than a critical analysis.

Books and Articles Touching on Becque

ANTOINE, ANDRÉ. *Mes Souvenirs sur le Théâtre-Libre.* Paris: Fayard, 1921.

BOUVIER, EMILE. "La Date de Composition des *Corbeaux,*" *Revue d'Histoire littéraire de la France.*[31] (January-March, 1924), 118-25. Maintains that Becque must have written *Les Corbeaux* in the spring of 1872 or 1873.

CARLSON, MARVIN. *André Antoine's "Memories of the Théâtre-Libre."* Coral Gables: University of Miami Press, 1964. A translation of Antoine's *Mes Souvenirs sur le Théâtre-Libre* with a short preface, index of names most frequently mentioned in the text, and photographs of writers of the Théâtre-Libre as well as of scenes from some of the plays.

CHANDLER, F. W. *The Contemporary Drama of France.* Boston, 1920. Claims that Becque, rather than Zola, pointed the way to Naturalism on the stage.

CIGOJ, BREDA. "Un Critique français trop peu connu: Henry Becque," *Revue d'Histoire littéraire de la France,* 62 (April-June, 1962), 241-63. Best discussion of Becque as a critic.

DUMESNIL, RENÉ. *Le Réalisme et le Naturalisme.* Paris: del Duca de Gigord, 1955. Denies the assumption that Becque is a Naturalist.

FILON, AUGUSTIN. *De Dumas à Rostand.* Paris: A. Colin, 1898. Trans. by C. J. Hogarth. New York, 1898 (out of print). Defines the *comédie rosse* and credits Becque with its creation in *La Parisienne.*

GASSNER, JOHN. *The Theater in Our Times.* New York: Crown, 1954. The best discussion of Becque's theater in English.

LEMAÎTRE, JULES. *Impressions de Théâtre (1888-1898),* III, X. Paris: Boivin et Cie. Chapters on Becque, originally published as separate reviews, show sympathetic understanding and enthusiasm.

MARTINO, PIERRE. Le Naturalisme (1870-1895). Paris: Armand Colin, 1923. Calls Becque the founder of the Naturalistic theater.

SARCEY, FRANCISQUE. *Quarante Ans de Théâtre,* I, VI. Paris: *Bibliothèque des Annales politiques et littéraires,* 1900. Chapters on Becque originally published as separate reviews in *Le Temps.* Admires Becque's dramatic skill but considers him too pessimistic and cynical.

SMITH, HUGH ALLISON. *Main Currents of Modern French Drama.* New York: Henry Holt, 1925. Claims that Becque first started comedy on its "famous Naturalistic orgy" in the days of the Théâtre-Libre.

STOCK, P. V. "Le Mémorandum d'un éditeur: Henry Becque anecdotique," *Mercure de France,* 258 (February-March, 1935), 44-62.

Index

(The works of Becque are listed under his name)